Learn Spanish In One Week

Copyright © 2023 Geoff Jackson

First publication March 2023

Learn Spanish In One Week

Chapters

Learn Spanish In One Week

Spanish Pronunciation

a =   This letter sounds like the *ah* sound you use to express realisation in English: "Ah" yes, you are so right!

b = This sounds like the English b as in belt, bell or brilliant.

c. = This sounds like the English k. When it is before "e" or "i" it sounds like "th" as in thirty. (Many parts of Spain use the "th" pronunciation while in other countries they will use a "s" sound.)

ch = This sounds like the "ch" as in chest.

d =. This sounds like the English d as in day

e = This sounds like "eh" when you use the phrase , "eh, what did you say?"

f =. This sounds like the English f as in friend.

g = This sounds like the English g as in game. If it comes before "e" or "i" it becomes a harsh h as in the Spanish word for people, "gente". Pronunciation = (hen-teh).

h = This word is usually silent.

i = This sounds like "ee" as in the words bee or sweet.

j = This letter is pronounced like the English "h" sound as in the Spanish word for July which is "julio. Pronunciation = (hoo-lee-oh)

k = Not used very often in Spanish but sounds the same as the English "k" as in king.

l = This is like the English "l" as in left.

Learn Spanish In One Week

ll = Sounds like the English y as in yellow. In Spanish yellow is "amarillo" (ah-mah-ree-yoh).

m = Like the English m as in mother.

n = Like the English n as in end or never.

ñ = This is a totally separate letter and sounds like "ny" in canyon or "ni" as in onion

o =. This sounds like the English o as in so, but a shorter sound as in the expression, "oh, I see".

p = This sounds like the English p as in people.

q = This letter sounds like the English k and is always followed by the letter u.

r = This is like the English r but with a slight roll of the tongue. At the beginning of a word you must make the sound more harsh and roll your tongue.

rr = This is a like the English r but very harsh and you must roll your tongue.

s =. This is the same as the English s as in snake.

t = This is the same at the English t as in table but it is pronounced a little softer.

u = This sounds like the English "oo" as in food.

v = This sounds like the English b as in ball. Spanish word for cow is "vaca" (bah-kah)

w = This sounds like the English w.

x = This is pronounced like the English k as in "locks"

y = This sounds like the English y as in yes

z =. In Spain this is pronounced like "th" as in the English word "this" but in other countries it sounds more like the English s.

When the pronunciation is displayed as "ah" - "eh" - "oh" - "th" follow sounds below

"ah" pronounced "ah" as in Africa. Spanish for "April":. =. "abril" (ah-breel)

"eh" pronounced "ay" as in "day" but not as harsh. Spanish for "where": = "donde" (don-deh)

"oh" pronounced "oh" as in "doe" but not as harsh. Spanish for "money": =. "dinero" (dee-neh-roh)

"th" pronounced "th" as in "thief". Spanish for "dinner": = "cena" (theh-nah)

Learn Spanish In One Week

Spanish Grammar

Nouns

All nouns, people, places, animals, things etc, have a gender (male or female).

Most masculine nouns end in"o" like el perro (the dog) or el banco (the bank) and the masculine word for "the" is "el". (When we show pronunciation in this book we won't be pronouncing the word for "the" as we would be repeating it all the time.)

Most feminine nouns end in "a" like la casa (the house) or la puerta (the door) and the feminine word for "the" is "la".

There are exceptions and you will learn these as you progress through the book.

To make a noun plural just add a "s" on the end. The word for "the" will change for masculine from "el" to "los" and for feminine from"la" to las". For example, the dog "el perro" will become "los perros" (the dogs) and the cow "la vaca" will become "las vacas" (the cows).

Adjectives

In Spanish, adjectives must agree with the nouns they are describing which means they must show if they are feminine or masculine and also singular or plural to match the noun. Also, the adjective always follows the noun. So a feminine example would be, "the red house" which is "la casa roja". When it becomes plural it changes to "the red houses" which is "las casas rojas". A masculine example is, "the white dog" which is "el perro blanco". When this becomes plural it changes and becomes, "the white dogs" which translates as "los perros blancos".

Indefinite Article

In Spanish the indefinite article has four forms all of which depend on whether the noun is masculine, feminine, singular or plural.

Un caballo (a horse)

Unos caballos (some horses)

Una vaca (a cow)

Unas vacas (some cows)

Learn Spanish In One Week

Adjectives

How it is pronounced

English	Spanish	Pronunciation
Aggressive	Agresivo	ah-greh-see-boh
Attractive	Atractivo	ah-trak-tee-boh
Bad	Malo	mah-loh
Bald	Calvo	kal-boh
Beautiful	Hermoso	er-moh-soh
Big	Grande	gran-deh
Cheap	Barato	bah-rah-toh
Chubby	Rechoncho	reh-chon-choh
Clean	Limpio	leem-pee-oh
Clever	Listo	lees-toh
Cold	Frío	free-oh
Clumsy	Torpe	tor-peh
Colossal	Colosal	koh-loh-sal
Delightful	Encantador	en-kan-tah-dor
Different	Diferente	dee-feh-ren-teh
Different	distinto	dees-teen-toh
Difficult	Dificil	dee-fee-theel
Dirty	Sucio	soo-thee-oh
Easy	Fácil	fah-theel
Expensive	Caro	kah-roh

Learn Spanish In One Week

How it is pronounced

English	Spanish	Pronunciation
Faithful	Fiel	fee-el
Famous	Famoso	fah-moh-soh
Fast	Rápido	rrah-pee-doh
Fat	Gordo	gor-doh
Fierce	Feroz	feh-roth
Flabby	Fofo	foh-foh
Funny	Gracioso	grah-thee-oh-soh
Gentle	Suave	swah-beh
Gigantic	Gigantesco	hee-gan-tess-koh
Good	Bueno	bweh-noh
Gorgeous	Precioso	preh-thee-oh-soh
Great	Estupendo	es-too-pen-doh
Great	Excelente	ehks-theh-len-teh
Handsome	Guapo	gwah-poh
Healthy	Saludable	sah-loo-da-bleh
High	Alto	al-toh
Honest	Honesto	oh-ness-toh
Hot	Caliente	ka-lee-en-teh
Interesting	Interesante	een-teh-reh-san-teh
Itchy	Irritado	ee-ree-tah-doh

Learn Spanish In One Week

How it is pronounced

English	Spanish	Pronunciation
Kind	Amable	ah-mah-bleh
Large	Grande	gran-deh
Lazy	Perezoso	peh-reh-thoh-soh
Little	Pequeño	peh-keh-nyoh
Little	Poco	poh-koh
Lively	Animado	ah-nee-mah-doh
Loud	Fuerte	fwer-teh
Loud	Ruidoso	rroo-ee-doh-soh
Low	Bajo	bah-hoh
Magnificent	Magnífico	mag-nee-fee-koh
Massive	Masivo	mah-see-boh
Narrow	Estrecho	es-treh-choh
Near	Cerca	ther-kah
New	Nuveo	nweh-boh
Obnoxious	Odioso	oh-dee-oh-soh
Old	Viejo	bee-eh-hoh
Polite	Educado	eh-doo-kah-doh
Poor	Pobre	poh-breh
Quiet	Tranquilo	tran-kee-loh
Repulsive	Repulsivo	reh-pool-see-boh

Learn Spanish In One Week

How it is pronounced

English	Spanish	Pronunciation
Rich	Rico	rree-koh
Scary	De miedo	deh-mee-eh-doh
Silent	Silencioso	see-len-thee-oh-soh
Short	Bajo	ba-hoh
Short	Corto	kor-toh
Skinny	Flaco	fla-koh
Slow	Despacio / lento	des-pah-thee-oh / len-toh
Small	Pequeño	peh-keh-nyoh
Very small	Muy pequeño	mwee-peh-keh-nyoh
Soft	Suave	swah-beh
Strong	Fuerte	fwer-teh
Tall	Alto	al-toh
Tiny	Minúsculo	mee-noos-koo-loh
Ugly	Feo	feh-oh
Warm	Cálido	ka-lee-doh
Wide	Ancho	an-choh
She is beautiful	Ella es hermosa	eh-yah-es-er-moh-sah
He is tall with short hair	Él es alto con pelo corto	el-es-al-toh-kon-peh-loh-cor-toh
The pillow is soft	La almohada es suave	la-al-moh-ah-da-es-swah-beh

Learn Spanish In One Week

Accessories

English	Spanish	Pronunciation
Backpack	La mochila	moh-chee-la
Belt	El cinturón	theen-too-ron
Bracelet	La pulsera	pool-seh-rah
Bracelet	El brazalete	brah-thah-leh-teh
Brush	El cepillo	theh-pee-yoh
Comb	El peine	peh-neh
Earring	El arete	ah-reh-teh
Earring	El pendiente	pen-dee-en-teh
Eye shadow	La sombra de ojos	som-bra-deh-oh-hohs
Glasses	Las gafas	gah-fas
Hair clip	La horqilla	or-kee-yah
Handbag / purse	La cartera	kar-teh-rah
Handbag / purse	El bolso	bol-soh
Hand cream	La crema de manos	kreh-mah-deh-mah-nos
Handkerchief	El pañuelo	pah-nweh-loh
Hat	El sombrero	som-breh-roh
Headscarf	El pañuelo	pah-nweh-loh
Lighter	El encendedor	en-thehn-deh-dor
Lipstick	El pintalabios	peen-tah-lah-bee-os
Lipstick	La barra de labios	bah-rrah-deh-lah-bee-os

Learn Spanish In One Week

English	Spanish	Pronunciation
Mascara	El rímel	rree-mel
Matches	Los fósforos	foss-foh-ross
Moisturiser	La crema hidratante	kreh-mah-ee-drah-tan-teh
Nail clippers	El cortaúñas	kor-tah-oo-nyass
Nail file	La lima	lee-mah
Nail polish	El esmalte	es-mal-teh
Nail polish	Esmalte de uñas	es-mal-teh-deh-oo-nyass
Perfume	El perfume	per-foo-meh
Ring	El anillo	ah-nee-yoh
Safety pin	El imperdible	eem-per-dee-bleh
Scarf	La bufanda	boo-fan-dah
Scissors	La tijera	tee-heh-rah
Tampons	El tampón	tam-pon
Tweezers	Las pinzas	peen-thahs
Umbrella	El paraguas	pah-rah-gwas
Wallet	La cartera	kar-teh-rah
Wedding ring	El anillo de casado	ah-nee-yoh-deh-ka-sa-doh
How much are these gloves	Cuánto cuestan estos guantes	kwan-toh-kwes-tan-es-tos-gwan-tehs
Put on your hat	Ponte tu sombrero	pon-teh-too-som-breh-roh
That's my umbrella	Ese es mi paraguas	eh-seh-es-mee-pah-rah-gwas

Learn Spanish In One Week

Airport

English	Spanish	Pronunciation
Air hostess	La azafata	ah-thah-fah-tah
Airline ticket	El billete de avión	bee-yeh-teh-deh-ah-bee-yon
Airplane	La avión	ah-bee-yon
Airport	El aeropuerto	ah-eh-roh-pwer-toh
Airport gate	Puerta de embarque	pwer-tah-deh-em-bar-keh
Arrivals	La llegada	yeh-gah-dah
Boarding gate	Puerta de embarque	pwer-tah-deh-em-bar-keh
Boarding pass	La tarjeta de embarque	tar-heh-tah-deh-em-bar-keh
Cancelled	Cancelado	kan-thell-ah-doh
Customs	La aduana	ah-dwan-ah
Currency exchange	El cambio de divisa	kam-bee-oh-deh-dee-bee-sah
Departures	Las salidas	sah-lee-das
Entrance	La entrada	en-trah-dah
Exit	La salida	sah-lee-dah
Flight	El vuelo	bweh-loh
Flight number	El número de vuelo	noo-meh-roh-deh-bweh-loh
Gate	La puerta	pwer-tah
Hand luggage	El equipaje de mano	eh-kee-pah-heh-deh-mah-noh
Information	La información	een-for-mah-thee-on
Late	Tarde	tar-deh

Learn Spanish In One Week

English	Spanish	Pronunciation
Lost	Perdido	per-dee-doh
Luggage	El quipaje	eh-kee-pah-heh
Luggage pickup	Recogida de equipaje	reh-koh-gee-dah-deh-eh-kee-pah-heh
Name	El nombre	nom-breh
Passenger	El pasajero	pah-sah-heh-roh
Passport	El pasaporte	pah-sah-por-teh
Passport please	Pasaporte por favor	pah-sah-por-teh-por-fah-bor
Security control	La control de seguridad	kon-trol-deh-seh-goo-ree-dad
Suitcase	La maleta	mah-leh-tah
Terminal	Terminal	ter-mee-nal
Can you help me?	¿Me puedes ayudar?	meh-pwer-dehs-ah-yoo-dar
Delayed flight	Vuelo retrasado	bweh-loh-reh-trah-sah-doh
Do you speak English?	¿Hablas inglés	ah-blass-eeng-lehs
I'm lost	Estoy perdido	es-toy-per-dee-doh
Is it a direct flight?	¿Es un vuelo directo?	es-oon-bweh-loh-dee-rek-toh
Is this seat taken?	¿Este asiento está ocupado?	es-teh-ah-see-en-toh-es-ta-oh-koo-pa-doh
Seat number	Número de asiento	noo-meh-roh-deh-ah-see-en-toh
Where is gate two?	¿Donde está la puerta dos?	don-deh-es-tah-la-pwer-tah-doss
Where's the toilet?	¿Donde está el baño?	don-deh-es-tah-el-bah-nyoh
Which way?	¿En qué dirección?	en-keh-dee-rek-thee-on

Learn Spanish In One Week

Animals

English	Spanish	Pronunciation
Alligator	El caimán	keye-man
Ant	La hormiga	or-mee-gah
Baboon	El babuino	bah-boo-ee-noh
Bear	El oso	oh-soh
Beatle	El escarabajo	es-kah-rah-bah-hoh
Bee	La abeja	Ah-beh-hah
Bird	El pájaro	pah-hah-roh
Butterfly	La mariposa	mah-ree-poh-sah
Camel	El camello	kah-meh-yoh
Cat	El gato	gah-toh
Caterpillar	La oruga	oh-roo-gah
Chicken	El pollo	poh-yoh
Chimpanzee	El chimpancé	cheem-pan-theh
Cockroach	El cucaracha	koo-kah-rah-cha
Cow	La vaca	bah-kah
Crab	El cangrejo	kan-greh-hoh
Crocodile	El cocodrilo	kok-oh-dree-loh
Dog	El perro	peh-rroh
Dolphin	El delfín	del-feen
Donkey	El burro	boo-rroh

Learn Spanish In One Week

English	Spanish	Pronunciation
Dragonfly	La libélula	lee-beh-loo-lah
Duck	El pato	pah-toh
Eagle	El águila	ah-gee-lah
Elephant	El elefante	eh-leh-fan-teh
Fish	El pez	peth
Flea	La pulga	pool-gah
Fly	La mosca	moss-kah
Fox	El zorro	zoh-rroh
Frog	La rana	rrah-nah
Giraffe	La jirafa	hee-rah-fah
Goat	La cabra	kah-brah
Goose	El ganso	gan-soh
Gorilla	El gorila	goh-ree-lah
Grasshopper	El saltamontes	sal-tah-mon-tehs
Hedgehog	El erizo	eh-ree-thoh
Hippopotamus	El hipopótamo	ee-poh-poh-ta-moh
Horse	El caballo	kah-bah-yoh
Hyena	La hiena	yeh-nah
Jellyfish	La medusa	meh-doo-sah
Kangaroo	El canguro	kan-goo-roh

Learn Spanish In One Week

English	Spanish	Pronunciation
Killer whale	La orca	or-kah
Ladybird	La mariquita	mah-ree-kee-tah
Leopard	El leopardo	leh-oh-par-doh
Lion	El león	leh-on
Lizard	El lagarto	lah-gar-toh
Lobster	La langosta	lan-goss-tah
Meerkat	La suricata	soo-ree-kah-tah
Monkey	El mono	moh-noh
Mosquito	El mosquito	moss-kee-toh
Mouse	El ratón	rah-ton
Octopus	El pulpo	pool-poh
Orangutan	El orangután	oh-rang-oo-tan
Ostrich	El avestruz	ah-bess-trooth
Otter	La nutria	noo-tree-ah
Panther	La pantera	pan-teh-rah
Parrot	El loro	loh-roh
Peacock	El pavo real	pah-boh-reh-al
Pelican	El pelícano	peh-lee-kah-noh
Penguin	El pingüino	peeng-gween-noh
Pig	El cerdo	ther-doh

Learn Spanish In One Week

English	Spanish	Pronunciation
Pigeon	La paloma	pah-loh-mah
Polar bear	El oso polar	oh-so-poh-lar
Rabbit	El conejo	koh-neh-hoh
Rat	El rata	rrah-tah
Rhinoceros	El rinoceronte	rree-noh-theh-ron-teh
Salmon	El salmón	sal-mon
Scorpion	El escorpión	es-kor-pee-yon
Sea horse	El caballito de mar	kah-bah-yee-toh-deh-mar
Sea lion	El león marino	leh-on-mah-ree-noh
Shark	El tiburón	tee-boo-ron
Sheep	La oveja	oh-beh-hah
Shrimp	El camarón	kah-mah-ron
Skunk	La mofeta	moh-feh-tah
Snail	El caracol	kah-rah-kol
Snake	La serpiente	ser-pee-en-teh
Spider	La araña	ah-rah-nyah
Squid	El calamar	kah-lah-mar
Squirrel	La ardilla	ar-dee-yah
Swan	El cisne	thees-neh
Tiger	El tigre	tee-greh

Learn Spanish In One Week

English	Spanish	Pronunciation
Tortoise	La tortuga	tor-too-gah
Turkey	El pavo	pah-boh
Walrus	La morsa	mor-sah
Whale	La ballena	bah-yeh-nah
Wasp	La avispa	ah-bees-pah
Wolf	El lobo	loh-boh
Zebra	La cebra	theh-brah
The big elephant	El gran elefante	el-gran-eh-leh-fan-teh
The elephant is big	El elefante es grande	el-eh-leh-fan-teh-es-gran-deh
The cat is black	El gato es negro	el gah-toh-es-neh-groh
A black cat	Un gato negro	oon-gah-toh-neh-groh
The snail is slow	El caracol es lento	el-kah-rah-kol-es-len-toh
The slow snail	El caracol lento	el-kah-rah-kol-len-toh
The mouse is small	El ratón es pequeño	el-rah-ton-es-peh-keh-nyoh
The small mouse	El ratón pequeño	el-rah-ton-peh-keh-nyoh
The fast eagle	El águila rápida	el-ah-gee-lah-rah-pee-dah
The eagle is fast	El águila es rápida	el-ah-gee-lah-es-rah-pee-dah
I like rabbits	Me gustan los conejos	meh-goo-stan-loss-kon-eh-hoss
I like this rabbit	Me gusta este conejo	meh-goo-stah-es-teh-kon-eh-hoh
I don't like this rabbit	No-me gusta este conejo	no-meh-goo-stah-es-teh-kon-eh-hoh

Learn Spanish In One Week

Bank

English	Spanish	Pronunciation
Account	La cuenta	kwen-tah
Account holder	Titular de la cuenta	teet-oo-lar-deh-la-kwen-ta
Account number	El número de cuenta	noo-meh-roh-deh-kwen-tah
Amount	El importe	eem-por-teh
Bank	El banco	ban-koh
Bank account	La cuenta bancaria	kwen-tah-ban-kah-ree-ah
Bank clerk	El empleado de banco	em-pleh-a-doh-deh-ban-koh
Cash	Dinero en efectivo	dee-neh-roh-en-eh-fek-tee-boh
Change	El cambio	kam-bee-oh
Charge	El cargo	kar-go
Cheque	El cheque	cheh-keh
Credit	El crédito	kreh-dee-toh
Credit card	La tarjeta de crédito	tar-heh-tah-deh-kreh-dee-toh
Currency	La moneda	moh-neh-dah
Current account	La cuenta corriente	kwen-tah-koh-rree-en-teh
Date	La fecha	feh-chah
Debit Card	La tarjeta de débito	tar-heh-tah-deh-deh-bee-toh
Debt	La deuda	deh-oo-dah
Exchange rate	El tipo de cambio	tee-poh-deh-kam-bee-oh
Expenses	Los gastos	gass-toss

Learn Spanish In One Week

English	Spanish	Pronunciation
Expiry date	La fecha de caducidad	feh-cha-deh-kah-doo-thee-dad
Fixed interest	Interés fijo	een-teh-ress-fee-hoh
Loan	El péstamo	press-tah-moh
Manager	El director	dee-rek-tor
Money	El dinero	dee-neh-roh
Mortgage	La hipoteca	ee-poh-teh-kah
Savings	Las ahorros	ah-oh-rross
Savings account	La cuenta de ahorros	kwen-tah-deh-a-oh-rross
Security guard	El / la guardia de seguridad	gwar-dee-a-deh-seh-goo-ree-dad
Security Number	El número de seguridad	noo-meh-roh-deh-seh-goo-ree-dad
Signature	La firma	feer-mah
Sign here	Firma aqui	feer-mah-ah-kee
Tax	El impuesto	eem-pwess-toh
Variable interest	Interés variable	een-teh-ress-bah-ree-ah-bleh
Is the bank open today?	¿Es el banco abierto hoy?	es-el-ban-koh-a-bee-er-toh-oy
I need a savings account	Necesito una cuenta de ahorros	neh-theh-see-toh-oo-na-kwen-tah-deh-ah-oh-rros
I want to transfer money	Quiero transferir dinero	kee-eh-roh-trans-fer-eer-dee-neh-roh
I would like to make a withdrawal	Me gustaría hacer un retiro	meh-goo-stah-ree-ah-ah-ther-oon-reh-tee-roh

Learn Spanish In One Week

Beach

English	Spanish	Pronunciation
Bay	La bahía	bah-ee-ah
Beach	La playa	pla-yah
Beach towel	La toalla de playa	toh-ah-yah-deh-pla-yah
Beautiful view	Vista hermosa	bees-tah-er-moh-sah
Boat	El barco	bar-koh
Coast	La costa	koss-tah
Help	Ayudar	ah-yoo-dar
Help me	Ayúdame	a-yoo-dah-meh
How much?	¿Cuánto?	kwan-toh
Ice cream	El helado	eh-la-doh
Island	La isla	ees-lah
Lifeguard	El / La salvavidas	sal-bah-bee-dass
Ocean view	Vista-al mar	bees-tah-al-mar
Port	El puerto	pwer-toh
Sand	La arena	ah-reh-nah
Sandy beach	La playa de arena	pla-yah-deh-ah-reh-nah
Sand castle	El castillo de arena	kass-tee-yoh-deh-ah-reh-nah
Sea	El mar	mar
Seagulls	Las gaviotas	gah-bee-oh-tass
Seaweed	El alga	al-gah

Learn Spanish In One Week

English	Spanish	Pronunciation
Shell	La concha	kon-chah
Sun	El sol	sol
Sunbathe	Tomar el sol	tom-ar-el-sol
Sunbed	La cama solar	kah-mah-soh-lar
Sunburn	La quemadura de sol	keh-mah-doo-rah-deh-sol
Sunscreen	El protector solar	proh-tek-tor-soh-lar
Sun glasses	Las gafas de sol	gah-fass-deh-sol
Sunny	Soleado	soh-leh-ah-doh
Sunset	El atardecer	ah-tar-deh-ther
Swim	Nadar	nah-dar
Swimming	La natación	nah-tah-thee-on
Swimming costume	La traje de baño	trah-heh-deh-ban-yoh
Towel	La toalla	toh-ah-yah
Umbrella	La paraguas	pah-rah-gwass
Can I swim here?	¿Puedo nadar aqui	pweh-doh-nah-dar-ah-kee
I want to go	Quiere ir	kee-er-oh-eer
I want to go swimming	Quiero ir a nadar	kee-eh-roh-eer-ah-nah-dar
The man is swimming	El hombre está nadando	el-om-breh-es-tah-na-dan-doh
The sand is hot	La arena está caliente	la-ah-reh-na-es-ta-ka-lee-en-teh
The water is cold	El agua está fría	el-ah-gwah-es-tah-free-ah

Learn Spanish In One Week

Body

English	Spanish	Pronunciation
Ankle	El tobillo	toh-bee-yoh
Anus	El ano	ah-noh
Appendix	El apéndice	ah-pen-dee-theh
Arm	El brazo	brah-thoh
Armpit	La axila	ak-see-lah
Artery	La arteria	ah-teh-ree-ah
Back	La espalda	es-pal-dah
Belly	El vientre	bee-en-treh
Biceps	El biceps	bee-thehps
Big toe	El dedo gordo	deh-doh-gor-doh
Bladder	La vejiga	beh-hee-gah
Blood	La sangre	san-greh
Blood vessel	El vaso sanguíneo	ba-soh-san-gee-neh-oe
Body	El cuerpo	kwer-poh
Bone	El hueso	weh-soh
Brain	El cerebro	theh-reh-broh
Breast	El seno	seh-noh
Bum / Backside	El trasero	trah-seh-roh
Buttocks	Las nalgas	nal-gas
Calf	El pantorrilla	pan-toh-rree-yah

Learn Spanish In One Week

English	Spanish	Pronunciation
Cheek	La mejilla	meh-hee-yah
Chest	El pecho	peh-choh
Chin	El mentón	men-ton
Chin	La barbilla	bar-bee-yah
Collarbone	La clavícula	klah-bee-koo-lah
Ear	El oreja	oh-reh-hah
Elbow	El codo	koh-doh
Eye	El ojo	oh-hoh
Eyebrow	La ceja	theh-hah
Eyelash	La pestaña	pess-tah-nyah
Eyelid	El párpado	par-pah-doh
Face	La cara	kah-rah
Feet	Los pies	pee-ehs
Finger	El dedo	deh-doh
Fist	El puño	poo-nyoh
Foot	El pie	pee-eh
Forearm	El antebrazo	an-teh-brah-thoh
Forehead	La frente	fren-teh
Freckle	La peca	peh-kah
Freckles	Las pecas	peh-kass

Learn Spanish In One Week

English	Spanish	Pronunciation
Genitals	Los genitales	heh-nee-tah-lehs
Groin	La ingle	een-gleh
Gum	La encía	en-thee-ah
Han	El mano	mah-noh
Hair	El pelo	peh-loh
Hamstring	El tendón de la corva	ten-don-deh-la-cor-bah
Head	La cabeza	kah-beh-thah
Heel	El talón	tah-lon
Hip	La cadera	kah-deh-rah
Jaw	La mandíbula	man-dee-boo-lah
Kidney	El riñón	rree-nyohn
Knee	La rodilla	rroh-dee-yah
Knuckle	El nudillo	noo-dee-yoh
Large intestine	El intestino grueso	een-tess-tee-noh-groo-weh-soh
Leg	La pierna	pee-er-nah
Ligament	El ligamento	lee-gah-men-toh
Lip	El labio	lah-bee-oh
Little finger	El meñique	meh-nyee-keh
Liver	El hígado	ee-gah-doh
Lung	El pulmón	pool-mon

Learn Spanish In One Week

English	Spanish	Pronunciation
Middle finger	El dedo medio	deh-doh-meh-dee-oh
Mouth	La boca	boh-kah
Muscle	El músculo	moos-koo-loh
Moustache	El bigote	bee-goh-teh
Nail	La uña	oo-nyah
Navel	El ombligo	om-blee-goh
Neck	El cuello	kweh-yoh
Nerves	Los nervios	ner-bee-oss
Nose	La nariz	nah-reeth
Nostril	El orificial nasal	oh-ree-fee-thee-al-nah-sal
Palm	La palma	pal-mah
Penis	El pene	peh-neh
Pelvis	La pelvis	pell-bees
Pupil	La pupila	poo-pee-lah
Rectum	El recto	rek-toh
Rib	La costilla	koss-tee-yah
Scalp	El cuero cabelludo	kweh-roh-kah-beh-yoo-doh
Shin	La espinilla	es-pee-nee-yah
Shoulder	El hombro	om-broh
Sideburn	La patilla	pa-tee-yah

Learn Spanish In One Week

English	Spanish	Pronunciation
Skin	El piel	pee-el
Skull	El cráneo	krah-neh-oh
Small intestine	El intestino delgado	een-tess-tee-noh-del-gah-doh
Sole	La planta	plan-tah
Spleen	El bazo	bah-thoh
Stomach	El estómago	es-toh-mah-goh
Teeth	Los dientes	dee-en-tehs
Tendon	El tendón	ten-don
Thigh	El muslo	moos-loh
Tibia	La tibia	tee-bee-ah
Throat	La garganta	gar-gan-tah
Thumb	El pulgar	pool-gar
Toe	El dedo del pie	deh-doh-del-pee-eh
Toenail	La uña del pie	oo-nyah-del-pee-eh
Tongue	La lengua	len-gwah
Tonsils	La amígdala	ah-meeg-dah-lah
Tummy	La barriga	bah-rree-gah
Vagina	La vagina	bah-hee-nah
Waist	La cintura	theen-too-rah
Wrist	La muñeca	moo-nyeh-kah

Learn Spanish In One Week

Buildings & Place

English	Spanish	Pronunciation
Amusement park	El parque de atracciones	par-keh-deh-ah-trak-thee-oh-nes
Art gallery	La galería de arte	ga-leh-ree-ah-deh-ar-teh
Bakery	La panadería	pah-nah-deh-ree-ah
Bank	El banco	ban-koh
Bar	El bar	bar
Bookstore	La librería	lee-breh-ree-ah
Bowling alley	Bolera	boh-leh-rah
Bridge	El puente	pwen-teh
Bus stop	La parada de autobús	pah-rah-dah-deh-ow-toh-boos
Bus terminal	La estación de autobuses	es-ta-thee-on-deh-ow-toh-boo-sehs
Car park	El estacionamiento	es-tah-thee-on-ah-mee-en-toh
Casino	El casino	kah-see-noh
Castle	El castillo	kass-tee-yoh
Cathedral	La catedral	kah-teh-dral
Cemetery	El cementerio	theh-men-teh-ree-oh
Chapel	La capilla	kah-pee-yah
Circus	El circo	theer-koh
Church	La iglesia	ee-gleh-see-ah
Clinic	La clínica	klee-nee-kah
Court	El tribunal	tree-boo-nal

Learn Spanish In One Week

English	Spanish	Pronunciation
Dam	La presa	preh-sah
Embassy	La embajada	em-bah-hah-dah
Factory	La fábrica	fah-bree-kah
Farm	La granja	gran-hah
Fire station	La estación de bomberos	es-ta-thee-on-deh-bom-beh-ross
Garage	La garaje	gah-rah-heh
Gymnasium	El gimnasio	heem-nah-see-oh
Hairdresser's	La peluquería	peh-loo-keh-ree-ah
Hospital	El hospital	os-pee-tal
House	La casa	kah-sah
Information office	Oficina de información	oh-fee-thee-na-deh-een-for-ma-thee-on
Jail	El cárcel	kar-thell
Kiosk	El quiosco	kee-oss-koh
Launderette	La lavandería automática	la-ban-deh-ree-ah-ow-toh-mah-tee-kah
Library	La biblioteca	bee-blee-oh-teh-kah
Lighthouse	El faro	fah-roh
Mall	El central comercial	thehn-troh-koh-mer-thee-al
Mansion	La mansión	man-see-on
Monastery	El monasterio	moh-nass-teh-ree-oh
Monument	El monumento	moh-noo-men-toh

Learn Spanish In One Week

English	Spanish	Pronunciation
Mosque	La mezquita	meth-kee-tah
Museum	El museo	moo-seh-oh
Nature reserve	La reserva natural	rreh-ser-bah-nah-too-ral
Neighbourhood	El barrio	bah-rree-oh
Office	La oficina	oh-fee-thee-nah
Optican's	La óptica	op-tee-kah
Palace	El palacio	pah-lah-thee-oh
Park	El parque	par-key
Petrol station	La gasolinera	gah-soh-lee-neh-rah
Pharmacy	La farmacia	far-mah-thee-ah
Police station	La estación de policía	es-tah-thee-on-deh-poh-lee-thee-ah
Post office	La oficina de correos	oh-fee-thee-nah-deh-koh-rreh-os
Prison	La prisión	pree-see-on
Pyramid	La pirámide	pee-rah-mee-deh
Restaurant	El restaurante	rrehs-tow-ran-teh
School	La escuela	es-kweh-lah
Sidewalk	La acera	ah-theh-rah
Skyscraper	El rascacielos	rass-kah-thee-eh-loss
Small town	El pueblo pequeño	pweh-bloh-peh-keh-nyoh
Sports Centre	El centro deportivo	thehn-troh-deh-por-tee-boh

Learn Spanish In One Week

English	Spanish	Pronunciation
Square	La plaza	plah-thah
Stadium	El estadio	es-tah-dee-oh
Street	La calle	kah-yeh
Street light	La farola	fah-roh-lah
Synagogue	La sinagoga	see-nah-goh-gah
Taxi rank	La parada de taxis	pah-rah-dah-deh-tak-sees
Temple	El templo	tem-ploh
Theatre	El teatro	teh-ah-troh
Toll road	La carretera de peaje	ka-rreh-teh-ra-deh-peh-ah-heh
Tower	La torre	toh-rreh
Town	El pueblo	pweh-bloh
Town / City	La ciudad	thee-oo-dad
Town hall	El ayuntamiento	ah-yoon-tah-mee-en-toh
Train station	La estación de tren	es-tah-thee-on-deh-tren
Tunnel	El túnel	too-nel
University	La universidad	oo-nee-ber-see-dad
Village	El pueblo	pweh-bloh
Windmill	El molino	moh-lee-noh
Youth hostel	El albergue juvenil	al-ber-geh-hoo-beh-neel
Zoo	El zoo	thoo

Learn Spanish In One Week

Car

English	Spanish	Pronunciation
Accelerator	El acelerador	ah-theh-leh-rah-dor
Antifreeze	El anticongelante	an-tee-kong-heh-lan-teh
Battery	La batería	bah-teh-ree-ah
Bonnet	El capó	kah-poh
Boot	El maletero	ma-leh-teh-roh
Brake	El freno	freh-noh
Brake light	La luz de freno	looth-deh-freh-noh
Car	El coche	coh-cheh
Clutch	El embrague	em-brah-geh
Danger	El peligro	peh-lee-groh
Dashboard	El salpicadero	sal-pee-kah-deh-roh
Engine	El motor	moh-tor
Exhaust	El escape	es-kah-peh
Gears	Las marchas	mar-chas
Glove compartment	La guantera	gwan-teh-rah
Handbrake	El freno de mano	freh-noh-deh-mah-noh
Headlight	El faro	fah-roh
Horn	El claxon	klak-son
Ignition	El encendido	en-thehn-dee-doh
Indicator	El intermitente	een-ter-mee-ten-teh

Learn Spanish In One Week

English	Spanish	Pronunciation
Key	La llave	ya-beh
Licence plate	La placa	plah-kah
Maximum speed	Velocidad máxima	beh-loh-thee-dad-max-ee-mah
Mirror	El espejo	es-peh-hoh
Motorway	La autopista	ow-tow-pees-tah
Oil	El aceite	ah-theh-teh
Per day	Por día	por-dee-ah
Per week	Por semana	por-seh-mah-nah
Petrol	La gasolina	gah-soh-lee-nah
Puncture	Un pinchazo	peen-cha-thoh
Radiator	La radiador	rrah-dee-ah-dor
Rear mirror	El espejo retrovisor	es-peh-hoh-reh-troh-bee-sor
Road works	Obras viales	oh-brass-bee-ah-lehs
Roof rack	La baca	bah-kah
Seats	Los asientos	ah-see-en-toss
Seat belt	El cinturón de seguridad	theen-too-ron-deh-seh-goo-ree-dad
Spark plug	La bujíc	boo-hee-ah
Steering wheel	El volante	boh-lan-teh
Suspension	La suspensión	soos-pen-see-on
Tyre	El neumático	neh-oo-mah-tee-koh

Learn Spanish In One Week

English	Spanish	Pronunciation
Wheel	La rueda	roo-eh-dah
Window	La ventanilla	ben-tah-nee-yah
Windscreen	El parabrisas	pah-rah-bree-sas
Windscreen wipers	El limpiaparabrisas	leem-pee-ah-pah-rah-bree-sas
Can I park here?	¿Puedo aparcar aquí?	pweh-doh-ah-par-car-ah-kee
Car accident	El accidente de coche	ak-thee-den-teh-deh-koh-cheh
Fill it up please	Llénalo por favor	yen-ah-loh-por-fah-bor
For how many days?	¿Por cuántos días?	por-kwan-toss-dee-ass
For how many weeks?	¿Por cuántos semanas?	por-kwan-toss-seh-man-ass
In the garage	En el garaje	en-el-gah-rah-heh
My car	Mi coche	mee-koh-cheh
My car is white	Mi coche es blanco	mee-koh-cheh-es-blan-koh
The tyre is flat	El neumático es plano	neh-oh-ma-tee-koh-es-pla-noh
This is my new car	Este es mi coche nuevo	es-teh-es-mee-coh-cheh-noo-eh-boh
Three days	Tres días	tres-dee-ass
Two weeks	Dos semanas	dos-seh-mah-nas
Unleaded please	Sin plomo por favor	seen-ploh-moh-por-fah-bor
What colour is your car?	¿De qué color es tu coche?	deh-keh-koh-lor-es-too-coh-cheh
Where's the car?	¿Dónde está el coche?	don-deh-es-tah-el-koh-cheh
Your car is fast	Tu coche es rápido	too-koh-cheh-es-rah-pee-doh

Learn Spanish In One Week

Clothes

English	Spanish	Pronunciation
Bathing suit	El traje de baño	trah-heh-deh-ban-yoh
Belt	El cinturón	theen-too-ron
Bikini	El bikini	bee-kee-nee
Blouse	La blusa	bloo-sah
Boots	Las botas	las-boh-tass
Bow tie	El corbatín	kor-bah-teen
Boxers	Los bóxers	loss-box-ers
Bra	El sostén	sos-ten
Button	El botón	boh-ton
Cap	La gorra	goh-rrah
Coat	El abrigo	ah-bree-goh
Camisole	La camisola	kah-mee-soh-lah
Cardigan	El cárdigan	kar-dee-gan
Clothes	La ropa	rroh-pah
Clothing	La ropa	rroh-pah
Cocktail dress	El vestido de cóctel	bes-tee-doh-deh-kok-tel
Corduroy	La pana	pah-nah
Cotton	El algodón	al-goh-don
Dress	El vestido	bes-tee-doh
Fur coat	El abrigo de piel	ah-bree-goh-deh-pee-el

Learn Spanish In One Week

English	Spanish	Pronunciation
Glasses	Las gafas	gah-fas
Glove	El guante	gwan-teh
Gloves	Los guantes	gwan-tehs
Hat	El sombrero	som-breh-roh
Hood	La capucha	kah-poo-chah
Jacket	La chaqueta	chah-keh-tah
Lace	El encaje	en-kah-heh
Leather	El cuero	kweh-roh
Long dress	El vestido largo	bes-tee-doh-lar-goh
Short dress	El vestido corto	bes-tee-doh-cor-toh
Loose	Holgado	ol-gah-doh
Mini skirt	La mini falda	mee-nee-fal-dah
Nightie	El camisón	kah-mee-son
Nylon	Nylon	neye-lon
Pyjamas	El pijama	pee-hah-mah
Pocket	El bolsillo	bol-see-yoh
Raincoat	El impermeable	eem-per-meh-ah-bleh
Sacrf	La bufanda	boo-fan-dah
Slippers	Las pantuflas	pan-too-flass
Sheepskin	El piel de oveja	pee-el-deh-oh-beh-hah

Learn Spanish In One Week

English	Spanish	Pronunciation
Shirt	La camisa	kah-mee-sah
Silk	La seda	seh-dah
Shoe	El zapato	thah-pah-toh
Shoes	Los zapatos	thah-pah-toss
Shorts	El short	short
Skirt	La falda	fal-dah
Sock	El calcetín	kal-theh-teen
Socks	Los calcetínes	kal-theh-teen-es
Stockings	Las medias	las-meh-dee-ass
Suit	El traje	trah-heh
Suspenders	Los tirantes	tee-ran-tehs
Sweater	El suéter	sweh-ter
Tie	La corbata	kor-bah-tah
Tight	Apretado	ah-preh-tah-doh
Thong	La tanga	tan-gah
Trousers / pants	Los pantalones	pan-tah-loh-nes
Trunks	El bañador	ban-yah-dor
T-Shirt	La camiseta	kah-mee-seh-tah
Underpants	Los calzones	loss-kal-thon-es
Underwear	La ropa interior	rroh-pah-een-teh-ree-or

Learn Spanish In One Week

English	Spanish	Pronunciation
Velvet	El terciopelo	ter-thee-oh-peh-loh
Wedding dress	El vestido de novia	bes-tee-doh-deh-noh-bee-ah
Wig	La peluca	peh-loo-kah
Wool	La lana	lah-nah
Bigger please	Más grande por favor	mass-gran-deh-por-fah-bor
Can I try this?	¿Puedo probar esto?	pweh-doh-proh-bar-es-toh
How much is this?	¿Cuánto cuesta esto?	kwan-tah-kwess-tah-es-toh
I don't like it	No me gusta	no-meh-goos-tah
I love your clothes	Me encanta tu ropa	meh-en-kan-tah-too-roh-pah
I want this one	Quiero este	kee-eh-roh-es-teh
I want two	Quiero dos	kee-eh-roh-dos
Smaller please	Más pequeño por favor	mass-peh-keh-nyoh-por-fa-bor
The black shirt	La camisa negra	kah-mee-sah-neh-grah
The white dress	El vestido blanco	bes-tee-doh-blan-koh
What colour?	¿De qué color?	deh-keh-koh-lor
What size	¿De qué talla?	deh-keh-tah-yah
Where is the changing room?	¿Dónde está el probador?	don-deh-es-ta-el-proh-bah-dor
With a hood	Con capucha	kon-kah-poo-chah
Without a hood	Sin capucha	seen-kah-poo-chah

Learn Spanish In One Week

Colours

English	Spanish	Pronunciation
Amber	ámbar	am-bar
Black	Negro	neh-groh
Blue	Azul	ah-thool
Brown	Marrón	mah-rron
Copper	Cobre	koh-breh
Dark brown	Marrón oscuro	mah-rron-os-koo-roh
Dark blue	Azul oscuro	ah-thool-os-koo-roh
Fuchsia	Fucsia	fook-see-ah
Gold	Dorado	doh-rah-doh
Grey	Gris	grees
Green	Verde	ber-deh
Indigo	índigo	een-dee-goh
Light blue	Azul claro	ah-thool-klah-roh
Lilac	Lila	lee-lah
Navy blue	Azul Marino	ah-thool-mah-ree-noh
Orange	Naranja	nah-ran-hah
Pink	Rosado	rroh-sah-doh
Purple	Morado	moh-rah-doh
Red	Rojo	rroh-hoh
Scarlet	Escarlata	es-kar-lah-tah

Learn Spanish In One Week

English	Spanish	Pronunciation
Silver	Plateado	pla-teh-ah-doh
Turquoise	Turquesa	toor-keh-sah
Violet	Violeta	bee-oh-leh-tah
White	Blanco	blan-koh
Yellow	Amarillo	ah-mah-ree-yoh
I don't like the red colour	No me gusta el color rojo	noh-meh-goos-tah-el-koh-lor-roh-hoh
I like the colour green	Me gusta el color verde	meh-goos-tah-el-koh-lor-ber-deh
The bicycle is blue	La bicicleta es azul	la-bee-thee-kleh-ta-es-ah-thool
The black door	La puerta negra	lah-pwer-tah-neh-grah
The blue table	La mesa azul	la-meh-sa-ah-thool
The dog is white	El perro es blanco	el-peh-rroh-es-blan-koh
The frog is green	La rana es verde	lah-rah-nah-es-ber-deh
The green apple	La manzana verde	lah-man-thah-nah-ber-deh
The green frog	La rana verde	lah-rah-nah-ber-deh
The pink bag	La bolsa rosada	lah-bol-sah-roh-sah-dah
The red house	La casa roja	lah-kah-sah-roh-hah
The white dog	El perro blanco	el-peh-rroh-blan-koh
The yellow car	El coche amarillo	el-koh-cheh-ah-mah-ree-yoh

Learn Spanish In One Week

Commands

English	Spanish	Pronunciation
Be a good boy	Sé un buen chico	seh-oon-bwen-chee-koh
Buy it	Cómpralo	kom-prah-loh
Click here	Haz clic aquí	ath-kleek-ah-kee
Close the door	Cierra la puerta	thee-eh-rrah-lah-pwer-tah
Close the window	Cierra la ventana	thee-eh-rrah-lah-ben-tah-nah
Come here	Ven aquí	ben-ah-kee
Come home	Ven a casa	ben-ah-kah-sah
Come in	Entra	en-trah
Come on	Ándale	an-dah-leh
Come on	Vamos	bah-moss
Come to my house	Ven a mi casa	ben-ah-me-kah-sah
Come with me	Venga conmigo	ben-gah-kon-mee-go
Don't be like that	No seas así	noh-seh-ass-ah-see
Don't do that	No hagas eso	noh-ah-gas-eh-soh
Don't eat	No coma	noh-koh-mah
Do not park here	No estacione aquí	noh-es-ta-thee-oh-neh-ah-kee
Don't run	No corras	noh-koh-rrass
Don't say anything	No digas nada	noh-dee-gas-nah-dah
Do not smoke	No. fume	noh-foo-meh
Don't speak	No hables	noh-ah-blehs

Learn Spanish In One Week

English	Spanish	Pronunciation
Don't tell me	No me digas	noh-meh-dee-gas
Don't write	No escriba	noh-es-kree-bah
Don't write to me	No me escribas	noh-meh-es-kree-bas
Eat	Coma	koh-mah
Forgive me	Perdóname	per-doh-nah-meh
Get dressed	Vistete	bees-teh-teh
Get out of here	Sal de aquí	sal-deh-ah-kee
Give it to me	Dámelo	dah-meh-loh
Go away	Vete	beh-teh
Help me	Ayúdame	ah-yoo-dah-meh
Just get dressed	Sólo vístete	soh-loh-bees-teh-teh
Let me pay	Déjame pagar	deh-hah-meh-pah-gar
Let's work	Trabajemos	trah-bah-heh-moss
Look	Mira	mee-rah
Make your bed	Haz tu cama	ath-too-kah-mah
Make the bed	Haz la cama	ath-lah-kah-mah
Please close the door	Por favor cierra la puerta	por-fa-bor-thee-eh-rrah-la-pwer-ta
Push	Empuje	em-poo-heh
Put it in my room	Ponlo en mi habitación	pon-loh-en-me-ah-bee-ta-thee-on
Read the book	Lee el libro	leh-eh-el-lee-broh

Learn Spanish In One Week

English	Spanish	Pronunciation
Shut up (informal)	Cállate	kah-yah-teh
Shut up (formal)	Cállese	kah-yar-seh
Sit down	Sentarse	sen-tar-seh
Sit down now	Sentarse ahora	sen-tar-seh-ah-oh-rah
Speak	Habla	ah-blah
Speak more slowly	Habla más lento	ah-blah-mas-len-toh
Stand up	Levántate	leh-ban-tah-teh
Stand up	Levantarse	leh-ban-tar-seh
Stop	Alto	al-toh
Stop it	Basta	bah-stah
Talk	Habla	ah-blah
Talk to me	Háblame	ah-blah-meh
Talk with me	Habla conmigo	ah-bla-con-mee-go
Tell me	Dime	dee-meh
Tell me how old you are	Dime cuántos años tiene	dee-meh-cwan-tos-an-yos-tee-en-eh
Wake up	Despiértate	des-pee-er-tah-teh
Watch out	Cuidado	kwee-dah-doh
Write	Escriba	es-kree-bah
Write the letter	Escriba la carta	es-kree-bah-lah-kar-tah
Write to me	Escríbeme	es-kree-beh-meh

Learn Spanish In One Week

Countries & Continents

English	Spanish	Pronunciation
Africa	Áfica	ah-free-kah
Antarctica	Antártida	an-tar-tee-dah
Asia	Asia	ah-see-ah
Australia	Australia	ows-tra-lee-ah
Europe	Europa	eh-oo-roh-pah
North America	América Del Norte	ah-meh-ree-ka-del-nor-teh
North America	Norteamérica	nor-teh-ah-meh-ree-kah
South America	América Del Sur	ah-meh-ree-kah-del-soor
South America	Sudamérica	sood-ah-meh-ree-kah
Albania	Albania	al-bah-nee-ah
Argentina	Argentina	ar-hen-tee-nah
Australia	Australia	ows-tra-lee-ah
Austria	Austria	ows-tree-ah
Belgium	Bélgica	bel-hee-kah
Brazil	Brasil	brah-seel
Bulgaria	Bulgaria	bool-gah-ree-ah
Cambodia	Camboya	kam-boh-yah
Canada	Canadá	kah-nah-dah
China	China	chee-nah
Colombia	Colombia	koh-lom-bee-ah

Learn Spanish In One Week

English	Spanish	Pronunciation
Costa Rica	Costa Rica	kos-tah-ree-kah
Croatia	Croacia	kroh-ah-thee-ah
Cyprus	Chipre	chee-preh
Denmark	Dinamarca	dee-nah-mar-kah
Egypt	Egipto	ee-heep-toh
England	Inglaterra	een-glah-teh-rrah
Ethiopia	Etiopía	eh-tee-oh-pee-ah
Finland	Finlandia	feen-lan-dee-ah
France	Francia	fran-thee-ah
Germany	Alemania	ah-leh-man-yah
Greece	Grecia	greh-thee-ah
Hungary	Hungría	oon-gree-ah
Iceland	Islandia	ees-lan-dee-ah
India	India	een-dee-ah
Indonesia	Indonesia	een-doh-neh-see-ah
Iran	Irán	ee-ran
Iraq	Iraq	ee-rak
Ireland	Irlanda	eer-lan-dah
Israel	Israel	ees-rrah-el
Italy	Italia	ee-ta-lee-ah

Learn Spanish In One Week

English	Spanish	Pronunciation
Jamaica	Jamaica	hah-may-kah
Lebanon	Líbano	lee-bah-noh
Libya	Libia	lee-bee-ah
Malaysia	Malasia	mah-lah-see-ah
Maldives	Maldivas	mal-dee-vas
Malta	Malta	mal-tah
Mexico	México	meh-hee-koh
Morocco	Marruecos	mah-rroo-eh-kos
Netherlands	Países Bajos	pah-ee-ses-bah-hos
Northern Island	Irlanda del Norte	eer-lan-dah-del-nor-teh
New Zealand	Nueva Zelanda	nweh-bah-theh-lan-dah
North Korea	Corea del Norte	koh-reh-ah-del-nor-teh
South Korea	Corea del Sur	koh-reh-ah-del-soor
Southern Island	Irlands del Sur	eer-lan-dah-del soor
Norway	Noruega	noh-ruh-weh-gah
Pakistan	Pakistán	pah-kees-tan
Philippines	Filipinas	fee-lee-pee-nas
Poland	Polonia	poh-loh-nee-ah
Portugal	Portugal	por-too-gal
Romania	Rumania	roo-mah-nee-ah

Learn Spanish In One Week

English	Spanish	Pronunciation
Russia	Rusia	rroo-see-ah
Saudi Arabia	Arabia Saudita	ah-rah-bee-ah-sow-dee-tah
Scotland	Escocia	es-koh-thee-ah
Singapore	Singapur	seen-gah-poor
South Africa	Sudáfrica	sood-ah-free-kah
Spain	España	es-pah-nya
Sweden	Suecia	sweh-tee-ah
Switzerland	Suiza	swee-thah
Syria	Siria	see-ree-ah
Thailand	Tailandia	tay-lan-dee-ah
Tunisia	Túnez	too-neth
Turkey	Turquía	toor-kee-ah
Ukraine	Ucrania	oo-kra-nee-ah
United Kingdom	Reino Unido	rrey-noh-oo-nee-doh
United States of America	Estados Unidos de América	es-ta-dos-oo-nee-dos-deh-ah-meh-ree-kah
Uruguay	Uruguay	oo-rr-gwah-ee
Vietnam	Vietnam	bee-et-nam
Wales	Gales	gah-lehs

Learn Spanish In One Week

Days of the Week

English	Spanish	Pronunciation
Monday	el lunes	loo-nehs
Tuesday	el martes	mar-tees
Wednesday	el miércoles	mee-er-koh-lehs
Thursday	el jueves	hweh-behs
Friday	el viernes	bee-er-nehs
Saturday	el sábado	sah-bah-doh
Sunday	el domingo	doh-meen-goh
This Saturday	Este sábado	es-teh-sah-bah-doh
Next Wednesday	El próximo miércoles	el-prok-see-moh-mee-er-koh-lehs
Week	La semana	seh-mah-nah
Next week	La próxima semana	la-prok-see-mah-seh-mah-nah
In one week	En una semana	en-oon-nah-seh-mah-nah
In two weeks	En dos semanas	en-dos-seh-mah-nas
Weekend	El fin de semana	feen-deh-seh-mah-nah
This weekend	Este fin de semana	es-teh-feen-deh-seh-mah-nah
Yesterday	Ayer	ah-yer
Tomorrow	Mañana	mah-nyah-nah
Morning	La mañana	lah-mah-nyah-nah
Tomorrow morning	Mañana por la mañana	ma-nyah-na-por-la-ma-nyah-nah
See you tomorrow	Hasta mañana	ass-tah-mah-nyah-nah

Learn Spanish In One Week

Dentist

English	Spanish	Pronunciation
Crown	La corona	koh-roh-nah
Dental bridge	Puente dental	pwen-teh-den-tal
Dental floss	El hilo dental	ee-loh-den-tal
Emergency	La emergencia	eh-mer-hen-thee-ah
Filling	El empaste	em-pas-teh
Fluoride	El fluoruro	floo-oh-roo-oh
Hygienist	Higienista	ee-hee-en-ees-tah
Infection	La infección	een-fek-thee-on
Injection	La inyección	een-yek-thee-on
Orthodontics	La ortodoncia	or-toh-don-thee-ah
Pain	El dolor	doh-lor
Receptionist	Recepcionista	rreh-thep-thee-on-nees-tah
Saliva	La saliva	sah-lee-bah
Teeth	Los dientes	dee-en-tehs
Tooth	El diente	dee-en-teh
Toothache	El dolor de muelas	doh-lor-deh-mweh-las
Toothbrush	El cepillo de dientes	theh-pee-yoh-deh-dee-en-tehs
Toothpaste	La pasta de dientes	pas-tah-deh-dee-en-tehs
Waiting room	La sala de espera	sah-lah-deh-es-peh-rah
Wisdom tooth	Muela de juicio	mweh-la-deh-hoo-ee-thee-oh

Learn Spanish In One Week

Directions

English	Spanish	Pronunciation
Across from	Enfrente de	en-fren-teh-deh
Across from the cathedral	Enfrente de la catedral	en-fren-teh-deh-la-ka-teh-dral
Ahead	Adelante	ah-deh-lan-teh
At the beginning of	Al comienzo de	al-kom-ee-en-thoh-deh
At the end of	Al final de	al-fee-nal-deh
At the end of the street	Al finale de la calle	al-fee-nal-deh-lah-kah-yeh
Avenue	La avenida	ah-beh-nee-dah
Behind	Atrás de	ah-tras-deh
Behind	Detrás de	deh-tras-deh
Behind the bank	Detrás del banco	deh-tras-del-ban-koh
Between	Entre	en-treh
Between the pharmacy and the library	Entre la farmacia y la biblioteca	en-treh-lah-far-ma-thee-ah-ee-lah-bee-blee-oh-teh-kah
Close	Cerca	ther-kah
Corner	La esquina	es-kee-nah
Do you have a map?	¿Tienes un mapa?	tee-en-ehs-oon-mah-pah
Down	Abajo	ah-bah-hoh
East	El este	es-teh
Entrance	La entrada	en-trah-dah
Exit	La salida	sah-lee-dah

Learn Spanish In One Week

English	Spanish	Pronunciation
Far	Lejos	leh-hoss
First on the left	Primero a la izquierda	pree-meh-roh-ah-la-eeth-kee-er-da
First on the right	Primero a la derecha	pree-meh-roh-ah-la-deh-reh-cha
Go straight ahead	Siga recto	see-gah-rek-toh
Go straight ahead	Siga derecho	see-gah-deh-reh-choh
Here	Aquí	ah-kee
How do I get	Cómo llego a	koh-moh-yeh-goh-ah
I don't know	No sé	noh-seh
I'm lost	Estoy perdido	es-toy-per-dee-doh
Inside	Adentro	ah-den-troh
Is it far?	¿Está lejos?	es-tah-leh-hoss
Is there?	¿Hay?	eye
Is there a bus?	¿Hay un autobús	eye-oon-ow-toh-boos
It's	Está	es-tah
It's here	Está aquí	es-tah-ah-kee
It's there	Está ahí	es-tah-ah-ee
It's near here	Está cerca de aquí	es-tah-ther-kah-deh-ah-kee
It's not far	No está lejos	noh-es-tah-leh-hoss
Keep straight	Sigue derecho	see-geh-deh-reh-choh
Left	Izquierda	eeth-kee-er-dah

Learn Spanish In One Week

English	Spanish	Pronunciation
Let's go	Vamos	bah-moss
Near	Cerca	ther-kah
Next to	Al lado de	ah-lah-doh-deh
Next to the school	Al lado de la escuela	ah-la-doh-deh-lah-es-kweh-lah
North	El norte	nor-teh
On	En	en
On the corner	En la esquina	en-lah-es-kee-nah
On the corner of	En la esquina de	en-lah-es-kee-nah-deh
On the left	A la izquierda	ah-lah-eeth-kee-er-dah
On the right	A la derecha	ah-lah-deh-reh-chah
Opposite	De enfrente	deh-en-fren-teh
Opposite	Opuesto	oh-pwes-toh
Outside	Afuera	ah-fweh-rah
Outside	Fuera	fweh-rah
Right	Derecha	deh-reh-chah
Roundabout	La glorieta	gloh-ree-eh-tah
Second on the left	Segundo a la izquierda	seh-goon-doh-a-la-eeth-kee-er-dah
Second on the right	Segundo a la derecha	seh-goon-doh-a-la-deh-reh-chah
Sidewalk	La acera	ah-theh-rah
Sidewalk	La banqueta	ban-keh-tah

Learn Spanish In One Week

English	Spanish	Pronunciation
South	El sur	soor
Straight	Derecho	deh-reh-choh
Straight ahead	Derecho	deh-reh-choh
Straight ahead	Todo recto	toh-doh-rek-toh
Street	La calle	kah-yeh
There	ahí	ah-ee
Third on the left	Tercero a la izquierda	ter-theh-roh-ah-la-eeth-kee-er-da
Third on the right	Tercero a la derecha	ter-theh-roh-ah-la-deh-reh-cha
To the left	A la izquierda	ah-lah-eeth-kee-er-dah
To the right	A la derecha	ah-lah-deh-reh-chah
Traffic light	El semáforo	seh-mah-foh-roh
Turn left	Gira a la izquierda	hee-rah-ah-la-eeth-kee-er-dah
Turn left	Gire a la izquierda	hee-reh-ah-la-eeth-kee-er-dah
Turn right	Gira a la derecha	hee-rah-ah-lah-deh-reh-chah
Turn right	Gire a la derecha	hee-reh-ah-lah-deh-reh-chah
Until	Hasta	ass-tah
West	El oeste	oh-es-teh
Where is?	¿Dónde está?	don-deh-es-tah
Where is the bank?	¿Dónde está el banco?	don-deh-es-ta-el-ba-koh
Where is the church?	¿Dónde está la iglesia?	don-deh-es-ta-la-ee-gleh-see-ah

Learn Spanish In One Week

Drinks

English	Spanish	Pronunciation
A bottle	Una botella	oo-nah-boh-teh-yah
A bottle of red wine	Una botella de vino tinto	oo-nah-boh-teh-yah-deh-bee-noh-teen-toh
A bottle of water	Una botella de agua	oo-na-boh-teh-ya-deh-ah-gwa
A bottle of wine	Una botella de vino	oo-na-boh-teh-ya-deh-bee-noh
A cold beer	Una cerveza fría	oo-nah-ther-beh-thah-free-ah
A glass of wine	Una copa de vino	oo-nah-koh-pah-deh-bee-noh
A glass of wine	Un vaso de vino	oo-bah-soh-deh-bee-noh
Apple juice	El jugo de manzana	hoo-goh-deh-man-thah-nah
Apple juice	El zumo de manzana	thoo-moh-deh-man-thah-nah
A small bottle of water	Una pequeña botella de agua	oo-nah-peh-keh-nyah-boh-teh-ya-deh-ah-gwah
Beer	La cerveza	ther-beh-thah
Black coffee	El café negro	kah-feh-neh-groh
Bottle	La botella	boh-teh-ya
Brandy	Brandy	bran-dee
Champagne	El champán	cham-pan
Coffee	El café	kah-feh
Coffee with milk	Café con leche	kah-feh-kon-leh-cheh
Coke	Coca Cola	koh-kah-koh-lah

Learn Spanish In One Week

English	Spanish	Pronunciation
Cold milk	Leche fría	leh-cheh-free-ah
Cold water	El agua fría	ah-gwah-free-ah
Drinks	Las bebidas	beh-bee-das
Do you want a drink?	¿Quieres una bebida?	kee-eh-rehs-oo-na-beh-bee-da
Fruit juice	El jugo de frutas	hoo-goh-deh-froo-tass
Fruit juice (Spain)	El zumo de frutas	thoo-moh-deh-froo-tass
Glass	La copa	koh-pah
Glass	El vaso	bah-soh
Grapefruit juice	El jugo de toronja	hoo-goh-deh-toh-ron-hah
Grapefruit juice	El zumo de toronja	thoo-moh-deh-toh-ron-hah
Hot chocolate	El chocolate caliente	choh-koh-la-teh-ka-lee-en-teh
Hot milk	Leche caliente	leh-cheh-kah-lee-en-teh
Hot water	El agua caliente	ah-gwa-kah-lee-en-teh
Ice	El hielo	yeh-loh
Juice	El jugo	hoo-goh
Juice	El zumo	thoo-moh
Lemonade	La limonada	lee-moh-nah-dah
Lots of ice please	Mucho hielo por favor	moo-choh-yeh-loh-por-fah-bor
Milk	La leche	leh-cheh
Orange juice	El jugo de naranja	hoo-goh-deh-nah-ran-hah

Learn Spanish In One Week

English	Spanish	Pronunciation
Orange juice	El zumo de naranja	thoo-moh-deh-nah-ran-hah
Red wine	El vino tinto	bee-noh-teen-toh
Rose wine	El vino rosado	bee-noh-rroh-sah-doh
Rum	El ron	rron
Sparkling wine	El vino espumoso	bee-noh-es-poo-moh-soh
Sugar	El / La azúcar	ah-thoo-kar
Tea	El té	teh
Tea with lemon	Té con limón	teh-kon-lee-mon
Tomato juice	El jugo de tomate	hoo-goh-deh-toh-mah-teh
Tomato juice	El zumo de tomate	thoo-moh-deh-toh-mah-teh
Two beers please	Dos cervezas por favor	doss-ther-beh-thas-por-fah-bor
Two cold beers please	Dos cervezas frías por favor	doss-ther-beh-thas-free-ass-por-fah-bor
Vodka	Vodka	bod-kah
Water	El agua	ah-gwah
What do you want to drink?	¿Qué quieres tomar?	keh-kee-eh-rehs-toh-mar
Whisky	Whisky	wees-kee
White wine	El vino blanco	bee-noh-blan-koh
Wine	El vino	bee-noh
With ice please	Con hielo por favor	kon-yeh-loh-por-fah-bor

Learn Spanish In One Week

Emotions

English	Spanish	Pronunciation
Angry	Enojado	eh-noh-hah-doh
Annoyed	Enojado	eh-noh-hah-doh
Bored	Aburrido	ah-boo-rree-doh
Brave	Valiente	bah-lee-en-teh
Calm	Calma	kal-mah
Depressed	Deprimido	deh-pree-mee-doh
Embarrassed	Avergonzado	ah-ber-gon-thah-doh
Emotional	Emocional	eh-moh-thee-oh-nal
Enthusiastic	Entusiasmado	en-too-see-ass-mah-doh
Excited	Emocionado	eh-moh-thee-oh-na-doh
Frustrated	Frustrado	froos-trah-doh
Furious	Furioso	foo-ree-oh-soh
Grumpy	Gruñón	groo-nyon
Guilty	Culpable	kool-pah-bleh
Happy	Feliz	feh-leeth
Helpless	Indefenso	een-deh-fen-soh
Horrified	Horrorizar	oh-rroh-ree-thar
Hungry	Hambriento	am-bree-en-toh
Inquisitive	Curioso	koo-ree-oh-soh
Inquisitive	Inquisitivo	een-kee-see-tee-boh

Learn Spanish In One Week

English	Spanish	Pronunciation
Insulted	Insultado	een-sool-tah-doh
Interested	Interesado	een-teh-reh-sah-doh
Jealous	Celoso	theh-loh-soh
Lonely	Solo	soh-loh
Lucky	Afortunado	ah-for-too-nah-doh
Mad	Enojado	eh-noh-hah-doh
Nervous	Nervioso	ner-bee-oh-soh
Offended	Ofendido	oh-fen-dee-doh
Pleased	Satisfecho	sah-tees-feh-choh
Proud	Orgulloso	or-goo-yoh-soh
Relaxed	Relajado	reh-lah-hah-doh
Remorseful	Arrepentido	ah-rreh-pen-tee-doh
Sad	Triste	trees-teh
Scared	Asustado	ah-soos-tah-doh
Sick	Enfermo	en-fer-moh
Shy	Tímido	tee-mee-doh
Stressed	Estresado	es-treh-sah-doh
Stupid	Estúpido	es-too-pee-doh
Surprised	Sorprendido	sor-pren-dee-doh
Tired	Cansado	kan-sah-doh

Learn Spanish In One Week

Family

English	Spanish	Pronunciation
Adult	El adulto	ah-dool-toh
Aunt	La tía	tee-ah
Bride	La novia	noh-bee-yah
Brother	El hermano	er-mah-noh
Brother-in-law	El cuñado	koo-nyah-doh
Children	Los niños	neen-yoss
Children	Las niñas	neen-yass
Cousin	El primo	pree-moh
Cousin	El prima	pree-mah
Dad	El papá	pah-pah
Daughter	La hija	ee-hah
Family	La familia	fah-mee-lee-ah
Father	El padre	pah-dreh
Father-in-law	El suegro	sweh-groh
Granddaughter	La nieta	nee-eh-tah
Grandfather	El abuelo	ah-bweh-loh
Grandmother	La abuela	ah-bweh-lah
Grandson	El nieto	nee-eh-toh
Groom	El novio	noh-bee-oh
Husband	El esposo	es-poh-soh

Learn Spanish In One Week

English	Spanish	Pronunciation
Mother	La madre	mah-dreh
Mother-in-law	La suegra	sweh-grah
Mum	La mamá	mah-mah
Nephew	El sobrino	soh-bree-noh
Niece	La sobrina	soh-bree-nah
Parents	Los padres	pah-drehs
Sister	La hermana	er-mah-nah
Sister-in-law	La cuñada	koo-nyah-dah
Son	El hijo	ee-hoh
Stepdaughter	La hijastra	ee-hass-trah
Stepfather	El padrastro	pa-drass-troh
Stepmother	La madrastra	mah-drass-trah
Stepson	El hijastro	ee-hass-tro
Uncle	El tío	tee-oh
Wife	La esposa	es-poh-sah
Woman / Wife	La mujer	moo-her
This is my daughter	Esta es mi hija	es-tah-es-mee-ee-hah
This is my husband	Este es mi esposo	es-teh-es-mee-es-poh-soh
This is my sone	Este es mi hijo	es-teh-es-mee-ee-hoh
This is my wife	Esta es mi esposa	es-tah-es-mee-es-poh-sah

Learn Spanish In One Week

Farm & Countryside

English	Spanish	Pronunciation
Barn	El granero	grah-neh-roh
Bucket	El cubo	koo-boh
Bee hive	La colmena	kol-meh-nah
Bull	El toro	toh-roh
Calf	El becerro / La becerra	beh-theh-roh / beh-theh-rah
Chicken	El pollo	poh-yoh
Crop	La cosecha	koh-seh-chah
Dairy farm	La granja lechera	gran-hah-leh-cheh-rah
Duckling	El patito	pah-tee-toh
Egg	El huevo	weh-boh
Foal	El potro	poh-troh
Farm	La granja	gran-hah
Farmer	El granjero	gran-heh-roh
Fence	La valla	bah-yah
Field	El campo	kam-poh
Gate	La puerta	pwer-tah
Goose	El ganso	gan-soh
Grass	El césped	thess-ped
Greenhouse	El invernadero	een-ber-nah-deh-roh
Hen	La gallina	gah-yee-nah

Learn Spanish In One Week

English	Spanish	Pronunciation
Horseshoe	La herradura	eh-rra-doo-rah
Hose	La manguera	man-geh-rah
Kitten	El gatito	gah-tee-toh
Lamb (under 1 year)	El cordero	kor-deh-roh
Lamb (over 1 year)	El borrego	boh-rreh-goh
Land	La tierra	tee-eh-rah
Mud	El barro	bah-rroh
Mule	La mula	moo-lah
On the farm	En la granja	en-lah-gran-hah
Piglet	El lechón	leh-chon
Rake	El rastrillo	rass-tree-yoh
Ram	El carnero	kar-neh-roh
Rooster	El gallo	gah-yoh
Scarecrow	El espantapájaros	es-pan-tah-pah-hah-rohs
Shovel	La pala	pah-lah
Soil	La tierra	tee-eh-rah
Stable	La cuadra	kwah-drah
Tractor	El tractor	trak-tor
Tree	El árbol	ahr-bol
Well	El pozo	poh-zoh

Learn Spanish In One Week

Flowers

English	Spanish	Pronunciation
Bark	La corteza	kor-teh-thah
Basket	La canasta	kah-nas-tah
Carnation	El clavel	klah-bell
Clippers	Las tijeras de podar	las-tee-heh-rass-deh-poh-dar
Compost	El abono orgánico	ah-boh-noh-or-gah-nee-koh
Daffodil	El narciso	nar-thee-soh
Daisy	La margarita	mar-gah-ree-tah
Fertiliser	El abono	ah-boh-noh
Flower	La flor	flor
Garden	El jardín	har-deen
Gardener	El jardinero	har-dee-neh-roh
Gardening	La jardinería	har-dee-neh-ree-ah
Hoe	La azada	ah-thah-dah
Hose	La manguera	man-geh-rah
Insecticide	El insecticida	een-sek-tee-thee-dah
Leaf	La hoja	oh-hah
Lily	El lirio	lee-ree-oh
Path	El camino	kah-mee-noh
Petal	El pétalo	peh-tah-loh
Pitchfork	La horca	or-kah

Learn Spanish In One Week

English	Spanish	Pronunciation
Plant	La planta	plan-tah
Plant pot	La maceta	mah-theh-tah
Pollen	El polen	poh-len
Rake	El rastrillo	rass-tree-yoh
Rock	La roca	rroh-kah
Root	La raíz	rrah-eeth
Rose	La rosa	rroh-sah
Seed	La semilla	seh-mee-yah
Shed	El cobertizo	koh-ber-tee-thoh
Spade	La pala	pah-lah
Sprinkler	El aspersor	as-per-sor
Stem	El tallo	tah-yoh
Sunflower	El girasol	hee-rah-sol
Trowel	La pala de jardinería	pa-la-deh-har-deen-eh-ree-ah
Tulip	El tulipán	too-lee-pan
Violet	La violeta	bee-oh-leh-tah
Watering can	La regadera	rreh-gah-deh-rah
Weed	La mala hierba	mah-lah-yer-bah
Wheelbarrow	La carretilla	kah-rreh-tee-yah
Worm	La lombriz	lom-breeth

Learn Spanish In One Week

Food

English	Spanish	Pronunciation
Almonds	Las almendras	al-men-dras
Bacon	El tocino	toh-thee-noh
Barbecue	La barbacoa	bar-bah-koh-ah
Beans	Las alubias	ah-loo-bee-ass
Beans	Los frijoles	free-hoh-lehs
Beef	La carne de vaca	kar-neh-deh-bah-kah
Beetroot	La remolacha	rreh-moh-lah-chah
Biscuit	La galleta	ga-yeh-tah
Black bean	Las alubias negras	ah-loo-bee-ass-neh-grass
Black pepper	La pimienta negra	pee-mee-en-tah-neh-grah
Black pudding	La morcilla	mor-thee-yah
Bread	El pan	pan
Bread crumb	La miga de pan	mee-gah-deh-pan
Breakfast	El desayuno	dess-ah-yoo-noh
Broad beans	Las habas	ah-bass
Broth	El caldo	kal-doh
Brown bread	El pan integral	pan-een-teh-gral
Butter	La mantequilla	man-teh-kee-yah
Cake	El pastel	pass-tel
Can	La lata	lah-tah

Learn Spanish In One Week

English	Spanish	Pronunciation
Casserole	La cazuela	kath-weh-lah
Cereal	Cereal	theh-reh-al
Cheese	El queso	keh-so
Cheesecake	La tarta de queso	tar-tah-deh-keh-soh
Chestnut	La castaña	kas-tah-nyah
Chicken	El pollo	poh-yoh
Chicken and rice	Arroz con pollo	ah-rroth-kon-poh-yoh
Chicken breast	Pechuga de pollo	peh-choo-gah-deh-poh-yoh
Chicken curry	El pollo al curry	poh-yoh-al-koo-rree
Chicken drumstick	El muslo de pollo	moos-loh-deh-poh-yoh
Chicken nugget	Patita de pollo	pa-tee-ta-deh-poh-yoh
Chick peas	La garbanzo	gar-ban-thoh
Cinnamon	La canela	kah-neh-lah
Clove of garlic	El diente de ajo	dee-en-teh-deh-ah-hoh
Cod	El bacalao	bah-kah-lah-oh
Cookie	La galleta	gah-yeh-tah
Corn flake	El copo de maíz	koh-poh-deh-mah-eeth
Crab	El cangrejo	kan-greh-hoh
Cream	La crema	kreh-mah
Cream	La nata	nah-tah

Learn Spanish In One Week

English	Spanish	Pronunciation
Cream cheese	El queso crema	keh-soh-kreh-mah
Crisps	Las patatas fritas	pah-tah-tass-free-tass
Cupcake	La magdalena	mag-dah-leh-nah
Dead	Muerto	mwer-toh
Delicious food	Comida rica	koh-mee-dah-ree-kah
Depression	La depresíon	deh-preh-see-on
Dessert	El postre	poss-treh
Diet	La dieta	dee-eh-tah
Dinner	La cena	theh-nah
Drink	La bebida	beh-bee-dah
Egg	El huevo	weh-boh
Egg cup	El huevera	weh-beh-rah
Egg white	La clara de huevo	kla-rah-deh-weh-boh
Evening meal	La cena	theh-nah
Exercise	El ejercicio	eh-her-thee-thee-oh
Fish	El pescado	pess-kah-doh
Flour	La harina	ah-ree-nah
Food / meal	La comida	koh-mee-dah
French fries	Las patatas fritas	pah-tah-tass-free-tass
Fried	Frito	free-toh

Learn Spanish In One Week

English	Spanish	Pronunciation
Frozen	Congelado	kon-heh-lah-doh
Garlic	El ajo	ah-hoh
Grated	Rallado	rah-yah-doh
Grated cheese	El queso rallado	keh-soh-rrah-yah-doh
Grease	La grasa	grah-sah
Green bean	Las judías verdes	hoo-dee-ass-ber-des
Green pepper	El pimiento verde	pee-mee-en-toh-ber-deh
Grill	La parrilla	pah-ree-yah
Grilled	A la plancha	ah-lah-plan-chah
Hake	La merluza	mer-loo-thah
Ham	El jamón	hah-mon
Handful	El puñado	poo-nyah-doh
Hard boiled egg	El huevo duro	weh-boh-doo-roh
Healthy	Saludable	sah-loo-dah-bleh
Heart	El corazón	koh-rah-thon
Herbs and spices	Hierbas y especias	ee-er-bass-ee-es-peh-thee-ass
Honey	La miel	mee-el
Ice cream	El herlado	eh-lah-doh
Icing sugar	El azúcar glas	ah-thoo-kar-glas
Hot dog	El perrito caliente	peh-rree-toh-ka-lee-en-teh

Learn Spanish In One Week

English	Spanish	Pronunciation
Lamb	El cordero	kor-deh-roh
Lard	La manteca	man-teh-kah
Lentils	La lenteja	len-teh-hah
Liver	El hígado	ee-gah-doh
Lunch	El almuerzo	al-mwer-thoh
Jam	La mermelada	mer-meh-lah-dah
Junk food	La comida basura	koh-mee-dah-bah-soo-rah
Marmalade	Mermelada de naranja	mer-meh-la-da-deh-na-ran-ha
Mayonnaise	La mayonesa	mah-yoh-neh-sah
Meal	La comida	koh-mee-dah
Meat	La carne	kar-neh
Meatball	La albóndiga	al-bon-dee-gah
Mince	La carne picada	kar-neh-pee-kah-dah
Mint	La menta	men-tah
Muffin	El mollete	moh-yeh-teh
Mustard	La mostaza	moss-tah-thah
Nut	La nuez	nweth
Nuts	Las nueces	noo-eh-thehs
Oil	El aceite	ah-theh-teh
Olive oil	Aceite de oliva	ah-theh-teh-deh-oh-lee-bah

Learn Spanish In One Week

English	Spanish	Pronunciation
Omelet	La tortilla	tor-tee-yah
Paella	La paella	pah-eh-yah
Peas	Los guisantes	gee-san-tehs
Peeled	Pelado	peh-lah-doh
Pepper	La pimienta	pee-mee-en-tah
Pizza	Pizza	pee-sah
Poached egg	El huevo escalfado	weh-boh-es-kal-fah-doh
Pork	El cerdo	ther-doh
Prawns	Las gambas	gam-bas
Raw	Crudo	kroo-doh
Recipe	La receta	reh-theh-tah
Recipe book	El recetario	reh-theh-tah-ree-oh
Red pepper	El pimiento rojo	pee-mee-en-toh-roh-hoh
Ribs	Las costillas	koss-tee-yass
Rice	El arroz	ah-rroth
Rice pudding	El arroz con leche	ah-rroth-kon-leh-cheh
Roast	El asado	ah-sah-doh
Salad	La ensalada	en-sah-lah-dah
Salt	La sal	sal
Salt and pepper	La sal y la pimienta	la-sal-ee-lah-pee-mee-en-tah

Learn Spanish In One Week

English	Spanish	Pronunciation
Salted	Salado	sah-lah-doh
Salty	Salado	sah-lah-doh
Sandwich	El bocadillo	boh-kah-dee-yoh
Sauce	La salsa	sal-sah
Sausage	La salchicha	sal-chee-chah
Seafood	Los mariscos	mah-ree-scoss
Skin	La piel	pee-el
Snack - picnic	La merienda	meh-ree-en-dah
Soup	La sopa	soh-pah
Sour	Agrio	ah-gree-oh
Spaghetti	El espagueti	es-pah-geh-tee
Spanish omelette	La tortilla de patatas	tor-tee-yah-deh-pah-tah-tas
Spicy	Picante	pee-kan-teh
Stale bread	Pan duro	pan-doo-roh
Stake	El bistec	bees-tek
Sugar	Azúcar	ah-thoo-kar
Sweet	Dulce	dool-theh
Sweet and sour	Agridulce	ah-gree-dool-theh
Tapas	Las tapas	tah-pas
Tart	La tarta	tar-tah

Learn Spanish In One Week

English	Spanish	Pronunciation
Tartar sauce	La salsa tártara	sal-sah-tar-tah-rah
Tasty food	Comida sabrosa	koh-mee-dah-sah-broh-sah
Temptation	La tentación	ten-tah-thee-on
Toast	La tostada	toss-tah-dah
Toasted	Tostado	toss-tah-doh
Tomato sauce	El kétchup	keh-choop
Tomato sauce	La salsa de tomate	sal-sah-deh-toh-mah-teh
Trout	La trucha	troo-chah
Tuna fish	El atún	ah-toon
Turkey	El pavo	pah-boh
Vanilla	La vainilla	beye-nee-yah
Veal	La ternera	ter-neh-rah
Vegetables	Las verduras	ber-doo-rass
Vegetarian	Vegetariano	beh-heh-tah-ree-ah-noh
Vinegar	El vinagre	bee-nah-greh
Whipped cream	La nata montada	nah-tah-mon-tah-dah
Yoghurt	El yogur	yoh-goor
Yolk	La yema	yeh-mah
I'm hungry	Tengo hambre	ten-goh-am-breh
The fridge is empty	La nevera está vacía	neh-beh-ra-es-ta-ba-thee-ah

Learn Spanish In One Week

Fruits

English	Spanish	Pronunciation
Apple	La manzana	man-thah-nah
Apricot	El albaricoque	al-ba-ree-koh-keh
Avocado	El aguacate	ah-gwa-kah-teh
Banana	La banana	bah-nah-nah
Blackberry	La mora	moh-rah
Blackcurrant	La grosella negra	groh-seh-yah-neh-grah
Blueberry	El arándano	ah-ran-dah-noh
Cherry	La cereza	theh-reh-thah
Coconut	El coco	koh-koh
Cucumber	El pepino	peh-pee-noh
Cranberry	El arándano agrio	ah-ran-dah-noh-ah-gree-oh
Date	El dátil	dah-teel
Fig	El higo	ee-goh
Gooseberry	La grosella espinosa	groh-seh-yah-es-pee-noh-sah
Grape	La uva	oo-bah
Grapefruit	La toronja	toh-ron-hah
Kiwi	Kiwi	kee-wee
Lemon	El limón	lee-mon
Lime	La lima	lee-mah
Lychee	El lichi	lee-chee

Learn Spanish In One Week

English	Spanish	Pronunciation
Mandarin	La mandarina	mah-dah-ree-nah
Mango	El mango	man-goh
Melon	El melón	meh-lon
Nectarine	La nectarina	nek-tah-ree-nah
Olive	La aceituna	ah-theh-too-nah
Orange	La naranja	nah-ran-hah
Papaya	La papaya	pah-pah-yah
Passion fruit	La maracuyá	mah-rah-koo-yah
Peach	El melocotón	meh-loh-koh-ton
Pear	La pera	peh-rah
Persimmon	El caqui	kah-kee
Pineapple	La piña	pee-nyah
Plum	La ciruela	thee-roo-eh-lah
Pomegranate	La granada	grah-nah-dah
Quince	El membrillo	mem-bree-yoh
Raspberry	La frambuesa	fram-bweh-sah
Strawberry	La fresa	freh-sah
Tangerine	La mandarina	man-dah-ree-nah
Tomato	El tomate	toh-mah-teh
Watermelon	La sandía	san-dee-ah

Learn Spanish In One Week

General Phrases

English	Spanish	Pronunciation
A bit	Un poco	oon-poh-koh
A bit more	Un poco más	oon-poh-koh-mass
According to me	Según yo	seh-goon-joh
All good	Todo bien	toh-doh-bee-en
All is well	Todo está bien	toh-doh-es-tah-bee-en
All the better	Todo lo mejor	toh-doh-loh-meh-hor
And you	Y tú	ee-too
And you	Y usted	ee-oos-ted
Are you busy?	¿Estás ocupado?	eh-stas-oh-koo-pah-doh
Are you ready?	Estás listo?	eh-stas-lee-stoh
A pleasure	Un gusto	oon-goo-stoh
A pleasure	Un placer	oon-plah-ther
Ask for help (formal)	Pida ayuda	pee-dah-ah-yoo-dah
Ask for help (informal)	Pide ayuda	pee-deh-ah-yoo-dah
At what time?	¿A qué hora?	ah-keh-oh-rah
Be careful	Tenga cuidado	ten-gah-kwee-dah-doh
Be careful	Ten cuidado	ten-kwee-dah-doh
Beat it / back off	Lárgate	lar-gah-teh
Best wishes	Saludos	sah-loo-doss
Bravo	Olé	oh-leh

Learn Spanish In One Week

English	Spanish	Pronunciation
Bye (formal)	Chao / chau	chow
Call me	Llámame	yah-mah-meh
Call me please	Llámame por favor	yah-mah-meh-por-fah-bor
Call the fire brigade	Llame a los bomberos	ya-meh-ah-loss-bom-beh-ross
Call the police	Llame a la policía	ya-meh-ah-la-pol-ee-thee-ah
Can I smoke?	¿Puedo fumar?	pweh-doh-foo-mar
Can I speak with?	¿Puedo hablar con?	pweh-doh-ab-lar-kon
Can I speak with you?	¿Puedo hablar con usted?	pweh-doh-ab-lar-kon-oo-sted
Can I taste it?	¿Puedo probarlo?	pweh-doh-proh-bar-loh
Can I use your phone?	¿Puedo usar su teléfono?	pweh-doh-oo-sar-soo-teh-leh-foh-noh
Can you believe it	Lo puedes creer	loh-pweh-des-kreh-er
Can you call me?	¿Puedes llamarme?	pweh-des-yah-mar-meh
Can you help me?	¿Me puedes ayudar?	meh-pweh-dehs-ah-yoo-dar
Can you help me?	¿Puedes ayudarme?	pweh-dehs-ah-yoo-dar-meh
Can you help me please?	¿Puedes ayudarme por favor?	pweh-dehs-ah-yoo-dar-meh-por-fa-bor
Can you repeat that?	¿Puedes repetirlo?	pweh-dehs-reh-peh-teer-loh
Can you speak more slowly?	¿Puedes hablar más despacio?	pweh-dehs-ah-blar-mass-des-pah-thee-oh
Can you translate this?	¿Puede traducir esto?	pweh-deh-tra-doo-theer-es-toh
Careful	Cuidado	kwee-dah-doh

Learn Spanish In One Week

English	Spanish	Pronunciation
Cheers	Salud	sah-lood
Close the door	Cierra la puerta	thee-eh-rah-lah-pwer-tah
Close the window	Cierra la ventana	thee-eh-rah-lah-ben-tah-nah
Come here	Ven aquí	ben-ah-kee
Come on	Vamos	bah-moss
Come on man	Venga hombre	ben-gah-om-breh
Come on children	Vamos niños	bah-moss-nee-nyoss
Congratulations	Enorabuena	en-oh-rah-bwen-ah
Congratulations	Felicidades	feh-lee-thee-dah-dehs
Congratulations	Felicitaciones	feh-lee-thee-tah-thee-oh-nehs
Delighted	Encantado	en-kan-tah-doh
Don't be silly	No seas tonto	no-seh-ass-ton-toh
Don't mention it	De nada	deh-nah-dah
Don't mention it	No hay de qué	noh-eye-deh-keh
Don't touch my phone	No toques mi teléfono	noh-toh-kehs-mee-teh-leh-foh-noh
Don't worry	No te preocupes	noh-teh-preh-oh-koo-pehs
Do you have? (formal)	¿Tiene?	tee-en-eh
Do you have? (informal)	¿Tienes?	tee-en-ehs
Do you have a car?	¿Tienes un coche?	tee-en-ehs-oon-coh-cheh
Do you have a dog?	¿Tienes un perro?	tee-en-ehs-oon-peh-rroh

Learn Spanish In One Week

English	Spanish	Pronunciation
Do you have any children?	¿Tienes hijos?	tee-en-ehs-ee-hoss
Do you have red wine?	¿Tienes vino tinto?	tee-en-ehs-bee-noh-teen-yoh
Do you like? (formal)	¿Le gusta?	leh-goos-tah
Do you like? (informal)	¿Te gusta?	teh-goos-tah
Do you like football?	¿Te gusta el fútbol?	teh-goos-tah-el-foot-bol
Do you like your job?	¿Te gusta tu trabajo?	teh-goos-tah-too-trah-bah-hoh
Do you need help?	¿Necesitas ayuda?	neh-theh-see-tass-ah-yoo-dah
Do you speak English?	¿Hablas inglés?	ah-blass-een-glehs
Do you understand?	¿Comprende? (formal)	kom-pren-deh
Do you understand?	¿Comprendes? (informal)	kom-pren-dehs
Do you understand?	¿Entiende? (formal)	en-tee-en-deh
Do you understand?	¿Entiendes? (informal)	en-tee-en-dehs
Do you understand English?	¿Entiende inglés?	en-tee-en-deh-een-glehs
Do you understand me?	¿Me entiendes?	meh-en-tee-en-dehs
Do you understand what I'm saying?	¿Entiende lo que digo?	en-tee-en-deh-loh-keh-dee-goh
Enjoy your meal	Qué aproveche	keh-ah-proh-beh-cheh
Enjoy your meal	Buen provecho	bwen-proh-beh-choh
Enough	Basta	bah-stah
Excuse me	Perdón	per-don

Learn Spanish In One Week

English	Spanish	Pronunciation
Excuse me	Disculpe	dees-kool-peh
Fire	Fuego	fweh-goh
Fine thanks	Bien gracias	bee-en-grah-thee-ass
For example	Poe ejemplo	por eh-hem-ploh
Get out of here	Fuera de aquí	fweh-rah-deh-ah-kee
Get out of here	Salte de aquí	sal-teh-deh-ah-kee
Get out of here	Vete de aquí	beh-teh-deh-ah-kee
Get well soon	Que te mejores pronto	keh-teh-meh-hor-ehs pron-toh
Go away	Vete	beh-teh
Go away, I don't want to see you	Vete, no quiero verte	beh-teh-noh-kee-eh-roh-ber-teh
Good	Bien	bee-en
Good	Bueno	bweh-noh
Good, and you?	¿Bien,y tu?	bee-en-ee-too
Good afternoon	Buenos tardes	bweh-nos-tar-dehs
Goodbye	Adiós	ah-dee-oss
Good day	Buen día	bwen-dee-ah
Good day	Buenos días	bweh-noss-dee-ass
Good evening	Buenas noches	bweh-nass-noh-chehs
Good luck	Buena suerte	bweh-nah-swer-teh

Learn Spanish In One Week

English	Spanish	Pronunciation
Good morning	Buenos días	bweh-noss-dee-ass
Good night	Buenas noches	bweh-nass-noh-chehs
Greetings	Saludos	sah-loo-doss
Happy anniversary	Feliz aniversario	feh-leeth-ah-nee-ber-sah-ree-oh
Happy birthday	Feliz cumpleaños	feh-leeth-koom-pleh-an-yoss
Happy Christmas	Feliz navidad	feh-leeth-nah-bee-dad
Happy day of the dead	Feliz Día de los Muertos	feh-leeth-dee-ah-deh-loss-mwer-toss
Happy Easter	Felices Pascuas	feh-lee-thehs-pass-kwass
Happy Hanukkah	Feliz Jánuca	feh-leeth-ha-noo-kah
Happy holidays	Felices fiestas	feh-lee-thehs-fee-es-tass
Happy Independence Day	Feliz Día de la Independencia	feh-leeth-dee-ah-deh-lah-een-deh-pen-den-thee-ah
Happy New Year	Feliz Año Nuevo	feh-leeth-an-yoh-nweh-boh
Happy Ramadan	Feliz Ramadán	feh-leeth-rah-mah-dan
Happy Saints Day	Feliz Santo	feh-leeth-san-toh
Happy Thanksgiving	Feliz Día de Acción de Gracias	feh-leeth-dee-ah-deh-ak-thee-on-deh-grah-thee-ass
Happy Valentines Day	Feliz día de los enamorados	feh-leeth-dee-ah-deh-loss-eh-nah-mor-ah-doss
Have a good holiday	Felices vacaciones	feh-lee-thehs-bah-kah-thee-on-ehs
Have a nice day	Qué tenga un buen día	keh-ten-gah-oon-bwen-dee-ah

Learn Spanish In One Week

English	Spanish	Pronunciation
Have a nice time	Qué lo pase bien	keh-loh-pah-seh-bee-en
Have a nice trip	Buen viaje	bwen-bee-ah-heh
He is right	Tiene razón	tee-eh-neh-rra-thon
Hello	Hola	oh-lah
Hello (on telephone)	Diga	dee-gah
Hello (on telephone)	Dígame	dee-gah-meh
Hello beautiful	Hola precioso	oh-lah-preh-thee-oh-soh
Hello, good day	Hola, buenos días	oh-lah-bweh-noss-dee-ass
Help	Auydar	ah-yoo-dar
Help	Socorro	soh-koh-rroh
Help us	Ayudarnos	ah-yoo-dar-noss
Here you are	Aquí tiene	ah-kee-tee-eh-neh
Hi	Hola	oh-lah
How about no	Qué tal si no	keh-tal-see-noh
How are you?	¿Cómo estás?	koh-moh-es-tass
How are your family?	¿Cómo está tu familia?	koh-moh-es-tah-too-fah-mee-lee-ah
How awful	Qué horrible	keh-oh-rree-bleh
How awful	Qué horror	keh-oh-rror
How can I help you?	¿En qué puedo ayudarle?	en-keh-pweh-doh-ah-yoo-dar-leh
How can I help you?	Cómo puedo ayudarte	koh-moh-pweh-doh-ah-yoo-dar-teh

Learn Spanish In One Week

English	Spanish	Pronunciation
How disgusting	Qué asco	keh-ass-koh
How do I go to	Cómo voy a	koh-moh-boy-ah
How do you say	Cómo se dice	koh-moh-seh-dee-theh
How do you spell that?	¿Cómo se escribe?	koh-moh-seh-eh-scree-beh
How does this work?	¿Cómo funciona esto?	koh-moh-foon-thee-on-ah-es-toh
How've you been?	¿Cómo te ha ido?	koh-moh-teh-ah-ee-doh
How's it going? (formal)	¿Cómo te va?	koh-moh-teh-bah
How's it going? (informal)	¿Cómo le va?	koh-moh-leh-bah
How's it going?	¿Qué tal?	keh-tal
How great / That's great	Qué bien	keh-bee-en
How lucky	Qué suerte	keh-swer-teh
How many children do you have?	¿Cuántos hijos tienes?	kwen-toss-ee-hohs-tee-en-ehs
How much?	¿Cuanto?	kwan-toh
How much does it cost?	¿Cuánto cuesta?	kwan-toh-kwess-tah
How much is it?	¿Cuánto es?	kwan-toh-es
How much is this?	¿Cuánto cuesta esto?	kwan-toh-kwess-tah-es-toh
How old are you?	¿Cuánto años tienes?	kwan-toh-ah-nyoss-tee-eh-nehs
How scary	Qué miedo	keh-mee-eh-doh
Hurry up	Date prisa	da-teh-pree-sah

Learn Spanish In One Week

English	Spanish	Pronunciation
I agree	Estoy de acuerdo	es-toy-deh-ah-kwer-doh
I already have plans	Ya tengo planes	ya-ten-goh-plah-nehs
I'm a little tired	Estoy un poco cansado	es-toy-oon-poh-koh-kan-sah-doh
I'm busy	Estoy ocupado	es-toy-oh-koo-pah-doh
I'm cold	Tengo frío	ten-goh-free-oh
I'm fine	Estoy bien	es-toy-bee-en
I'm fine thanks	Estoy bien gracias	es-toy-bee-en-gra-thee-ass
I'm Geoff	Yo soy Geoff	yoh-soy-jef
I'm fed up / I'm sick of	Estoy harto de	es-toy-ar-toh-deh
I'm fed up of studying	Estoy harto de estudiar	es-toy-ar-toh-deh-es-too-dee-ar
I'm from England	Soy de Inglaterra	soy-deh-een-glah-teh-rrah
I'm from Liverpool	Soy de Liverpool	soy-deh-lee-ber-pool
I'm going	Me voy	meh-boy
I'm going home	Estoy yendo a casa	es-toy-yen-doh-ah-kah-sah
I'm going home	Me voy a casa	meh-boy-ah-kah-sah
I'm going on a trip	Me voy de viaje	meh-boy-deh-bee-ah-heh
I'm going to be late	Voy a llegar tarde	boy-ah-yeh-gar-tar-deh
I'm going to bed	Me voy a la cama	meh-boy-ah-lah-kah-mah
I am going to sleep	Voy a dormir	boy-ah-dor-meer
I'm going to the beach	Voy a la playa	boy-ah-lah-plah-yah

Learn Spanish In One Week

English	Spanish	Pronunciation
I'm going to think about it	Voy a pensarlo	boy-ah-pen-sar-loh
I'm good	Estoy bien	es-toy-bee-en
I'm good thanks	Estoy bien, gracias	es-toy-bee-en-grah-thee-ass
I'm good thanks, and you?	Estoy bien gracias. ¿Y tu?	es-toy-bee-en-grah-thee-ass-ee-too
I'm good at	Se me da bien	seh-meh-dah-bee-en
I'm good at cooking	Se me da bien cocinar	seh-meh-dah-bee-en-koh-thee-nar
I'm hungry	Tengo hambre	ten-goh-am-breh
I'm in a hurry	Tengo prisa	ten-goh-pree-sah
I'm just kidding	Estoy bromeando	es-toy-brom-eh-an-doh
I'm lost	Estoy perdido	es-toy-per-dee-doh
I'm not sure	No estoy seguro	noh-es-toy-seh-goo-roh
I am proud of you	Estoy orgullosa de ti	es-toy-or-goo-yoh-soh-deh-tee
I'm sick	Estoy enfermo	es-toy-en-fer-moh
I'm sleepy	Tengo sueño	ten-goh-sweh-nyoh
I'm sorry	Disculpe	dees-kool-peh
I'm sorry	Lo siento	loh-see-en-toh
I'm very sorry	Lo siento mucho	loh-see-en-toh-moo-choh
I'm thirsty	Tendo sed	ten-goh-sed
I am thirty years old	Tengo treinta años	ten-goh-trehn-tah-an-yoss
I'm tired	Estoy cansado	es-toy-kan-sah-doh

Learn Spanish In One Week

English	Spanish	Pronunciation
I'm vegetarian	Soy vegetariano	soy-beh-heh-tah-ree-ah-noh
I'm very glad to see you	Estoy muy contento de verte	es-toy-mwee-kon-ten-toh-deh-ber-teh
I'm well thank you	Estoy bien gracias	es-toy bee-en-grah-thee-ass
I am working	Estoy trabajando	es-toy-trah-bah-han-doh
I am working tomorrow	Estoy trabajando mañana	es-toy-trah-bah-han-doh-man-yah-nah
I believe that	Creo que	kreh-oh-keh
I can't	No puedo	no-pweh-doh
I can't complain	No puedo quejarme	no-pweh-doh-keh-har-meh
I can't go out	No puedo salir	no-pweh-doh-sah-leer
I can't hear you	No puedo escucharte	no-pweh-doh-es-koo-char-teh
I can't remember	No me acuerdo	noh-meh-ah-kwer-doh
I can't remember	No puedo recordar	no-pweh-doh-reh-kor-dar
I can't wait	No puedo esperar	no-pweh-doh-es-peh-rar
I don't believe that	No creo que	noh-kreh-oh-keh
I don't believe you	No te creo	noh-teh-kreh-oh
I don't have	No tengo	noh-ten-goh
I don't know	No sé	noh-seh
I don't like	No me gusta	noh-meh-goos-tah
I don't mind	Me da igual	meh-dah-ee-gwal
I don't speak English	No hablo inglés	noh-ah-bloh-een-glehs

Learn Spanish In One Week

English	Spanish	Pronunciation
I don't speak Spanish	No hablo español	noh-ah-bloh-es-pah-nyoll
I don't think so	Creo que no	kreh-oh-keh-noh
I don't understand	No entiendo	noh-en-tee-en-doh
I don't understand	No comprendo	noh-kom-pren-doh
I don't understand Spanish	No entiendo español	noh-en-tee-en-doh-es-pah-nyoll
I don't understand you	No te entiendo	noh-teh-en-tee-en-doh
I don't want it	No lo quiero	noh-loh-kee-eh-roh
I don't want that	No quiero eso	noh-kee-eh-roh-eh-soh
I don't want to see you	No quiero verte	noh-kee-eh-roh-ber-teh
I don't want you here	No te quiero aquí	noh-teh-kee-eh-roh-ah-kee
If you don't like it	Si no te gusta	see-noh-teh-goo-stah
If you don't like it, there's the door	Si no te gusta,ahí está la puerta	see-noh-teh-goo-stah-ah-ee-es-tah-lah-pwer-tah
I feel angry	Me siento enojado	meh-see-en-toh-eh-noh-ha-doh
I feel good	Me siento bien	meh-see-en-toh-bee-en
I feel good today	Hoy me siento bien	oy-meh-see-en-toh-bee-en
I feel that	Siento que	see-en-toh-keh
I feel that something is wrong	Siento que algo está mal	see-en-toh-keh-al-goh-es-tah-mal
I forgot	Me olvidé	meh-ohl-bee-deh
I forgot	Se me olvidó	seh-meh-ohl-bee-doh

Learn Spanish In One Week

English	Spanish	Pronunciation
I forgot my keys	Me olvidé las llaves	meh-ohl-bee-deh-las-jah-behs
I've been robbed	Me han robado	meh-an-roh-bah-doh
I've had enough	He tendido bastante	ee-teh-nee-doh-bas-tan-teh
I have no idea	No tengo idea	noh-ten-goh-ee-deh-ah
I have three children	Tengo tres hijos	ten-goh-trehs-ee-hohs
I have to go	Me tengo que ir	meh-ten-goh-keh-eer
I have to go now	Me tengo que ir ahora	meh-ten-goh-keh-eer-ah-oh-rah
I hope not	Espero que no	es-peh-roh-keh-noh
I just want a snack	Sólo quiero una merienda	soh-loh-kee-eh-roh-oo-nah-meh-ree-en-dah
I like	Me gusta	meh-goos-tah
I like going to	Me gusta ir a	meh-goos-tah-eer-ah
I like going to the beach	Me gusta ir a la playa	meh-goos-tah-eer-ah-la-plah-yah
I like this	Me gusta esto	meh-goos-tah-es-toh
I like this music	Me gusta esta música	meh-goos-tah-es-tah-moo-see-kah
I like this song	Me gusta esta canción	meh-goos-tah-es-tah-kan-thee-on
I live in	Vivo en	bee-boh-en
I live in England	Vivo en Inglaterra	bee-boh-en-een-glah-teh-rrah
I love it	Me encanta	meh-en-kan-tah
I love you	Te amo	teh-ah-moh

Learn Spanish In One Week

English	Spanish	Pronunciation
I love you	Te quiero	te-kee-eh-roh
I miss you	Te echo de menos	teh-eh-choh-deh-meh-noss
I need a favour	Necesito un favor	neh-theh-see-toh-oon-fa-bor
I need help	Necesito ayuda	neh-theh-see-toh-ah-yoo-dah
I need to go home	Necesito ir a casa	neh-theh-see-toh-eer-ah-kah-sah
I need to lie down	Necesito tumbarme	neh-theh-see-toh-toom-bar-meh
I speak English	Hablo inglés	ah-bloh-een-glehs
I speak Spanish	Hablo español	ah-bloh-es-pan-yoll
I speak very little Spanish	Hablo muy poco español	ah-bloh-mwee-poh-koh-es-pan-yoll
I think it's very good	Creo que es muy bueno	kreh-oh-keh-es-mwee-bweh-noh
I think it's very good	Pienso que es muy bueno	pee-en-soh-keh-es-mwee-bweh-noh
I think it tastes very good	Creo que sabe bien	kreh-oh-keh-sah-beh-bee-en
I think I love you	Creo que te quiero	kreh-oh-keh-teh-kee-eh-roh
I think so	Creo que sí	kreh-oh-keh-see
I think that	Pienso que	pee-en-soh-keh
I want	Quiero	kee-eh-roh
I want a taxi	Quiero un taxi	kee-eh-roh-oon-tak-see
I want a ticket	Quiero un billete	kee-eh-roh-oon-bee-yeh-teh
I want more	Quiero más	kee-eh-roh-mass

Learn Spanish In One Week

English	Spanish	Pronunciation
I was born in	Nací en	nah-thee-en
I was born in England	Nací en Inglaterra	nah-thee-en-een-glah-teh-rrah
I understand	Entiendo	en-tee-en-doh
I understand	Comprendo	kon-pren-doh
I'll be with you in a second	Estoy contigo en un segundo	es-toy-kon-tee-goh-en-oon-seh-goon-doh
I wish you all the best	Te deseo todo lo mejor	teh-deh-seh-oh-toh-doh-loh-meh-hor
I'd like / I would like	Me gustaría	meh-goos-tah-ree-ah
I'd like more water	Me gustaría más agua	meh-goos-tah-ree-ah-mass-ah-gwah
If it were possible	Si fuera posible	see-fweh-rah-poh-see-bleh
In fact	De hecho	deh-eh-choh
In the morning	Por la mañana	por-la-man-yah-nah
In my opinion	A mi juicio	ah-mee-hoo-ee-thee-oh
In my opinion	En mi opinión	en-mee-oh-pee-nee-yon
Is it expensive?	¿Es caro?	es-kah-roh
Is it expensive?	¿Está caro?	es-tah-kah-roh
Is it fun?	¿Es divertido?	es-dee-ber-tee-doh
Is it good?	¿Es bueno?	es-bweh-noh
Is it good?	¿Está bien	es-tah-bee-en
Is it possible?	¿Es posible?	es-poh-see-bleh
Is it safe?	¿Es seguro?	es-seh-goo-roh

Learn Spanish In One Week

English	Spanish	Pronunciation
Is it to the left?	¿Está a la izquierda?	es-tah-ah-lah-eeth-kee-er-dah
Is it to the right?	¿Está a la derecha?	es-tah-ah-lah-deh-reh-chah
Is it true?	¿Es cierto?	es-thee-er-toh
Is it true?	¿Es verdad?	es-ber-dad
Is there anything else?	¿Hay algo más?	eye-al-goh-mass
Is there a problem?	¿Hay algún problema?	eye-al-goon-proh-bleh-mah
It doesn't matter	No importa	noh-eem-port-tah
It doesn't matter	No importa nada	noh-eem-port-tah-nah-dah
It's a pleasure	Es un placer	es-oon-plah-ther
It's expensive	Es caro	es-kah-roh
It is late / It's late	Es tarde	es-tar-deh
It's not important	No importa	noh-eem-port-tah
It's very annoying	Es muy molesto	es-mwee-moh-leh-stoh
It is very bad	Es muy malo	es-mwee-mah-loh
It is very beautiful	Es muy hermoso	es-mwee-er-moh-soh
It's very big	Es muy grande	es-mwee-gran-deh
It's very cheap	Es muy barato	es-mwee-bah-rah-toh
It's very expensive	Es muy caro	es-mwee-kah-roh
It's very noisy	Hay mucho ruido	eye-moo-choh-roo-ee-doh
It's very urgent	Es muy urgente	es-mwee-oor-hen-teh

Learn Spanish In One Week

English	Spanish	Pronunciation
It scares me	Me da miedo	meh-dah-mee-eh-doh
It seems to me that	Me parece que	meh-pah-reh-theh-keh
Just a little	Solo un poco	soh-loh-oon-poh-koh
Kiss me	Bésame	beh-sah-meh
Leave me alone	Déjame en paz	deh-hah-meh-en-path
Let me see	Déjame ver	deh-hah-meh-ber
Let me think	Déjame pensar	deh-hah-meh-pen-sar
Let's go	Vamos / Vámonos	bah-moss / ba-moh-noss
Let's see	Vamos a ver	bah-moss-ah-ber
Listen to me	Escúchame	es-kooch-ah-meh
Look at me	Mírame	meer-ah-meh
Lots of luck	Mucha suerte	moo-chah-swer-teh
Madam / Mrs	La señora	seh-nyor-rah
Maybe	Tal vez	tal-beth
Maybe later	Tal vez más tarde	tal-beth-mass-tar-deh
Maybe tomorrow	Tal vez mañana	tal-beth-man-yah-nah
Me too	Yo también	yoh-tam-bee-en
Merry Christmas	Feliz Navidad	feh-leeth-nah-bee-dad
Mine	Mío / mía	mee-oh / mee/ah
Miss	La señorita	seh-nyor-ree-tah

Learn Spanish In One Week

English	Spanish	Pronunciation
More please	Más por favor	mass-por-fah-bor
My name is	Me llamo	meh-yah-moh
My name is	Mi nombre es	mee-nom-breh-es
My Spanish is bad	Mi español es malo	mee-es-pah-nyoll-es-mah-loh
Next time	La próxima vez	lah-prok-see-mah-beth
Nice to meet you (male)	Encantado de conocerte	en-kan-tah-doh-deh-kon-oh-ther-teh
Nice to meet you (female)	Encantada de conocerte	en-kan-tah-dah-deh-kon-oh-ther-teh
Nice to meet you	Mucho gusto	moo-choh-goos-toh
No	No	noh
Not now	Ahora no	ah-oh-rah-noh
No problem	No hay problema	noh-eye-proh-bleh-mah
No problem	No hay de qué	noh-eye-deh-keh
No thank you	No gracias	noh-grah-thee-ass
No way	Qué va	keh-bah
Not so good	No muy bien	noh-mwee-bee-en
Not yet	Todavía no	toh-dah-bee-ah-noh
Nothing	Nada	nah-dah
Nothing else	Nada más	nah-dah-mass
Occasionally	De vez en cuando	deh-beth-en-kwan-doh

Learn Spanish In One Week

English	Spanish	Pronunciation
Of course	Claro	klah-roh
Of course	Claro que sí	klah-roh-keh-see
Of course not	Claro que no	klah-roh-keh-noh
Ok babe	Está bien amor	es-tah-bee-en-ah-mor
Once again	Otra vez	oh-trah-beth
One moment please	Un momento por favor	oon-moh-men-toh-por-fah-bor
On the other hand	Por otro lado	por-oh-troh-lah-doh
Only a little	Solo un poco	soh-loh-oon-poh-koh
Only for a moment	Sólo un momento	soh-loh-oon-moh-men-toh
Over here	Por aquí	por-ah-kee
Over there	Por ahí	por-ah-ee
Pardon	Perdón	per-don
Pardon	Perdone	per-doh-neh
Please	Por favor	por-fah-bor
Please be quiet	Silencio por favor	see-len-thee-oh-por-fah-bor
Please be quiet (Shut it)	Cállate por favor	kah-yah-teh-por-fah-bor
Pleased to meet you	Mucho gusto	moo-choh-goos-toh
Quick	Rápido	rrah-pee-doh
Quickly	Rápidamente	rrah-pee-dah-men-teh
Really	De veras	deh-beh-rass

Learn Spanish In One Week

English	Spanish	Pronunciation
Really	De verdad	deh-ber-dad
Run, hurry up	Corre date prisa	koh-reh-dah-teh-pree-sah
See you in the morning	Nos vemos en la mañana	noss-beh-moss-en-lah-man-yah-nah
See you tonight	Te veo esta noche	teh-beh-oh-es-tah-noh-cheh
See you	Hasta luego	ass-tah-lweh-goh
See you	Nos vemos	noss-beh-moss
See you later	Hasta luego	ass-tah-lweh-goh
See you Monday	Hasta el lunes	ass-tah-el-loo-nehs
See you next week	Hasta la semana que viene	ass-tah-lah-seh-mah-nah-keh-bee-en-eh
See you soon	Hasta pronto	ass-tah-pron-toh
See you tomorrow	Hasta mañana	ass-tah-man-yah-nah
Shut the door	Cerrar la puerta	theh-rar-lah-pwer-tah
Shut up	Cállate	kah-yah-teh
Sir	El señor	seh-nyor
Sit down	Sentarse	sen-tar-seh
Sit here	Siéntate aquí	see-en-tah-teh-ah-kee
So so	Así así	ah-see-ah-see
So so	Más o menos	mass-oh-meh-noss
So what	Y qué	ee-keh

Learn Spanish In One Week

English	Spanish	Pronunciation
Sorry	Lo siento	loh-see-en-toh
Sorry about that	Lo siento	loh-see-en-toh
Sorry I don't understand	Lo siento no entiendo	loh-see-en-toh-noh-en-tee-en-doh
Speak more slowly	Hablar más despacio	ah-blah-mass-des-pah-thee-oh
Speak slowly	Hablar despacio	ah-blah-des-pah-thee-oh
Stand up	Levantarse	leh-ban-tar-seh
Thank you for everything	Gracias por todo	grah-thee-ass-por-toh-doh
Thanks for the food	Gracias por la comida	grah-thee-ass-por-lah-koh-mee-dah
Thanks for your help	Gracias por tu ayuda	grah-thee-ass-por-too-ah-yoo-dah
Thank you / Thanks	Gracias	grah-thee-ass
Thanks very much	Muchas gracias	moo-chass-grah-thee-ass
That's enough	Es suficiente	es-soo-fee-thee-en-teh
That's enough	Ya basta	yah-bass-tah
That's expensive	Eso es caro	es-oh-es-kah-roh
That's very expensive	Eso es muy caro	es-oh-es-mwee-kah-roh
That's right	Así es	ah-see-es
That way please	Por allí por favor	por-ah-yee-por-fah-bor
The movie starts at seven	La película empieza a las siete	lah-peh-lee-koo-lah-em-pee-eh-thah-ah-lass-see-eh-teh
The pleasure is mine	El gusto es mío	el-goos-toh-es-mee-oh

Learn Spanish In One Week

English	Spanish	Pronunciation
There's the door	Ahí está la puerta	ah-ee-es-tah-lah-pwer-tah
There is / there are	Hay	eye
There isn't / there aren't	No hay	noh-eye
There is a lot to do	Hay mucho que hacer	eye-moo-choh-keh-ah-ther
There isn't a problem	No hay problema	noh-eye-proh-bleh-mah
Thief	Ladrón	lah-dron
This does not work	Esto no funciona	es-toh-noh-foon-thee-on-ah
This is a	Este es un	es-teh-es-oon
This is a	Esta es una	es-tah-es-oonah
This is a	Esto es un / una	es-toh-es-oon / oonah
This is very delicious	Esto es muy delicioso	es-toh-es-mwee-deh-lee-thee-oh-soh
This is very difficult	Esto es muy difícil	es-toh-es-mwee-dee-fee-theel
This is very important	Esto es muy importante	es-toh-es-mwee-eem-por-tan-teh
This way	Por aquí	por-ah-kee
This way please	Por aquí por favor	por-ah-kee-por-fah-bor
Today was bad	Hoy fue malo	oy-fweh-mah-loh
Two beers please	Dos cervezas por favor	doss-ther-beh-thass-por-fah-bor
Very cheap	Muy barato	mwee-bah-rah-toh
Very expensive	Muy caro	mwee-kah-roh
Very good	Muy bien	mwee-bee-en

Learn Spanish In One Week

English	Spanish	Pronunciation
Very good thank you	Muy bien gracias	mwee-bee-en-grah-thee-ass
Very well	Muy bien	mwee-bee-en
Watch out	Cuidado	kwee-dah-doh
Watch out	Ojo	oh-hoh
We're going home	Nos vamos a casa	noss-bah-moss-ah-kah-sah
We are going to be late	Vamos a llegar tarde	bah-moss-ah-yeh-gar-tar-deh
We are going to eat	Vamos a comer	bah-moss-ah-koh-mer
We're going to have dinner	Vamos a cenar	bah-moss-ah-theh-nah
We are going to the beach	Vamos a la playa	bah-moss-ah-la-plah-yah
We like it a lot	Nos gusta mucho	noss-goo-stah-moo-choh
We need a doctor	Necesitamos un médico	neh-theh-see-tah-moss-oon-meh-dee-koh
We will see	Vamos a ver	bah-moss-ah-ber
Welcome	Bienvenido	
Welcome everyone	Bienvenidos a todos	bee-en-beh-nee-doss-ah-toh-doss
Welcome to my home	Bienvenido a mi casa	bee-en-beh-nee-doh-ah-mee-kah-sah
Well done	Bien hecho	bee-en-eh-choh
What a pity	Qué lástima	keh-lass-tee-mah
What a shame	Qué lástima	keh-lass-tee-mah

Learn Spanish In One Week

English	Spanish	Pronunciation
What a surprise	Qué sorpresa	keh-sor-preh-sah
What are you doing?	¿Qué haces?	keh-ah-thehs
What are you doing?	¿Qué estás haciendo?	keh-es-tass-ah-thee-en-doh
What are you doing this weekend?	¿Qué haces este fin de semana?	keh-ah-thehs-es-teh-feen-deh-seh-mah-nah
What are you doing tonight?	¿Qué haces esta noche?	keh-ah-thehs-es-tah-noh-cheh
What do you study?	¿Qué estudias?	keh-es-too-dee-ass
What do you think?	¿Qué piensas?	keh-pee-en-sas
What do you think about this?	¿Qué piensas de esto?	keh-pee-en-sas-deh-es-toh
What do you want?	¿Qué quieres?	keh-kee-eh-rehs
What do you want to do?	¿Qué quieres hacer?	keh-kee-eh-rehs-ah-ther
What does that mean?	¿Qué significa eso?	keh-seeg-nee-fee-kah-es-oh
What does this mean?	¿Qué significa esto?	keh-seeg-nee-fee-kah-es-toh
What for?	¿Para que?	pah-rah-keh
What happened?	¿Qué pasó?	keh-pah-soh
What's happening?	¿Qué está sucediendo?	keh-es-tah-soo-theh-dee-en-doh
What's happening?	¿Qué pasa?	keh-pah-sah
What's his name?	¿Cómo se llama?	koh-moh-seh-yah-mah
What's the date?	¿Cuál es la fecha?	kwal-es-lah-feh-chah

Learn Spanish In One Week

English	Spanish	Pronunciation
What's your address?	¿Cuál es tu dirección?	kwal-es-too-dee-rek-thee-on
What is your telephone number?	¿Cuál es tu número de teléfono?	kwal-es-too-noo-meh-roh-deh-teh-leh-foh-noh
What is this?	¿Qué es esto?	keh-es-es-toh
What is this for	¿Para qué es esto?	pah-rah-keh-es-es-toh
What is that?	¿Qué es eso?	keh-es-es-oh
What is that for?	¿Para qué es eso?	pah-rah-keh-es-es-oh-
What's your job?	¿Cuál es tu trabajo?	kwal-es-too-trah-bah-hoh
What's your job?	¿En qué trabajas?	en-keh-trah-bah-hass
What's your favourite colour?	¿Cuál es tu color favorito?	kwal-es-too-koh-lor-fah-boh-ree-toh
What is your name?	¿Cuál es tu nombre?	kwal-es-too-nom-breh
What's your name (informal)	¿Cómo te llamas?	koh-moh-teh-yah-mass
What's your name (formal)	¿Cómo se llama?	koh-moh-seh-yah-mah
What's the matter?	¿Qué pasa?	keh-pah-sah
What's up?	¿Qué tal?	keh-tal
What's up? / What's going on?	¿Qué pasa?	keh-pah-sah
What time do you close?	¿A qué hora cierran?	ah-keh-oh-rah-thee-eh-rran
What time does the movie start?	¿A qué hora empieza la película?	ah-keh-oh-rah-em-pee-eh-thah-lah-peh-lee-koo-lah

Learn Spanish In One Week

English	Spanish	Pronunciation
When are we leaving?	¿Cuándo nos vamos?	kwan-doh-noss-bah-moss
When does the movie start?	¿Cuándo empieza la película?	kwan-doh-em-pee-eh-thah-lah-peh-lee-koo-lah
When will I see you?	¿Cuándo le veo?	kwen-doh-leh-beh-oh
Where are we?	¿Dónde estamos?	don-deh-es-tah-moss
Where are you from?	¿De dónde eres?	deh-don-deh-eh-ress
Where are you going?	¿A dónde vas?	ah-don-deh-bass
Where can I find?	¿Dónde puedo encontrar?	don-deh-pweh-doh-en-kon-trar
Where do you live?	¿Dónde vives?	don-deh-bee-behs
Where have you been?	¿Dónde has estado?	don-deh-ass-es-tah-doh
Where is?	¿Dónde está?	don-deh-es-tah
Where is my book?	¿Dónde está mi libro?	don-deh-es-tah-mee-lee-broh
Where is everyone?	¿Dónde están todos?	don-deh-es-tan-toh-dos
Where is my telephone?	¿Dónde está mi teléfono?	don-deh-es-tah-mee-teh-leh-foh-noh
Where is the bathroom?	¿Dónde está el baño?	don-deh-es-tah-el-bah-nyoh
Where is the bank?	¿Dónde está el banco?	don-deh-es-tah-el-ban-koh
Where is dad?	¿Dónde está papá?	don-deh-es-tah-pah-pah
Where is my husband?	¿Dónde está mi esposo?	don-deh-es-tah-mee-es-poh-soh
Where is my husband?	¿Dónde está mi marido?	don-deh-es-tah-mee-mah-ree-doh
Where is my mum?	¿Dónde está mi madre?	don-deh-es-tah-mee-mah-dreh

Learn Spanish In One Week

English	Spanish	Pronunciation
Where's my wife?	¿Dónde está mi esposa?	don-deh-es-tah-mee-es-poh-sah
Where's my wife?	¿Dónde está mi mujer?	don-deh-es-tah-mee-moo-her
Where were you born?	¿Dónde naciste?	don-deh-nah-thees-teh
Which one do you like?	¿Cuál te gusta?	kwal-teh-goos-tah
Which one is mine?	¿Cuál es el mío?	kwal-es-el-mee-oh
Who is she?	¿Quién es ella?	kee-en-es-eh-yah
Who is there?	¿Quién está ahí?	kee-en-es-tah-ah-ee
Who is this?	¿Quién es este?	kee-en-es-es-teh
With pleasure	Con mucho gusto	kon-moo-choh-goos-toh
Would you like to dance with me?	¿Te gustaría bailar conmigo?	teh-goo-stah-ree-ah-beye-lar-kon-mee-goh
Why not	Por qué no	por-keh-noh
Yes	Sí	see
You're in the way	Estorbas	es-tor-bass
You're welcome	De nada	deh-nah-dah
You can call me	Puedes llamarme	pweh-des-yah-mar-meh
You can choose	Puedes escoger	pweh-des-es-koh-her
You can come	Puedes venir	pweh-des-beh-neer
You can do it	Sí se puede	see-seh-pweh-deh
Yours faithfully / Yours sincerely	Atentamente / Saludos cordiales	ah-ten-tah-men-teh / sah-loo-dos-kor-dee-ah-lehs

Learn Spanish In One Week

Hobbies

English	Spanish	Pronunciation
Athletics	El atletismo	at-leh-tees-moh
Baseball	El Beisbol	behs-bol
Basketball	El baloncesto	bah-lon-thehs-toh
Board games	El juego de mesa	hweh-goh-deh-meh-sah
Chess	El ajedrez	ah-heh-dreth
Cooking	La cocina	koh-thee-nah
Cycling	El ciclismo	thee-klees-moh
Dancing	El baile	beye-leh
Darts	El dardos	dar-dohs
During the week	Durante la semana	doo-ran-teh-lah-seh-mah-nah
During the week I like to jog	Durante la semana me gusta correr	doo-ran-teh-lah-seh-mah-nah-meh-goos-tah-koh-rrer
Fishing	La pesca	pes-kah
Football	El fútbol	foot-bol
Free time	El tiempo libre	tee-em-poh-lee-breh
Gardening	La jardinería	har-dee-neh-ree-ah
Golf	El golf	golf
He / she likes	Le gusta	leh-goos-tah
Hiking	El excursionismo	eks-koor-see-on-nees-moh
Hiking	El senderismo	sen-deh-rees-moh

Learn Spanish In One Week

English	Spanish	Pronunciation
Hobby	El pasatiempo	pah-sah-tee-em-poh
Horse riding	La equitación	eh-kee-tah-thee-on
Hunting	La caza	kah-thah
I'm interested in	Me interesa	meh-een-teh-reh-sah
I don't like	No me gusta	noh-meh-goos-tah
I don't like cricket	No me gusta el cricket	noh-meh-goos-tah-el-kree-ket
I don't like sports	No me gusta los deportes	noh-meh-goos-tah-los-deh-por-tehs
I like	Me gusta	meh-goos-tah
I like ………. a lot	Me gusta ………mucho	meh-goos-tah-moo-choh
I like reading	Me gusta leer	meh-goos-tah-leh-er
I like swimming	Me gusta nadar	meh-goos-tah-nah-dar
I like to colour	Me gusta colorear	meh-goos-tah-koh-loh-reh-ar
I like to go shopping	Me gusta ir de compras	meh-goos-tah-eer-deh-kom-prass
I like to play	Me gusta jugar	meh-goos-tah-hoo-gar
I like to run	Me gusta correr	meh-goos-tah-koh-rer
I love	Me encanta	meh-en-kan-tah
I love running	Me encanta correr	meh-en-kan-tah-koh-rer
In my free time	En mi tiempo libre	en-mee-tee-em-poh-lee-breh
Listening to music	Escuchar música	es-koo-char-moo-see-kah
My hobbies are	Mis pasatiempos son	mees-pah-sah-tee-em-pohs-son

Learn Spanish In One Week

English	Spanish	Pronunciation
My favourite hobby is	Mi pasatiempo favorito es	mee-pah-sah-tee-em-poh-fah-boh-ree-toh-es
Photography	La fotografía	foh-toh-grah-fee-ah
Reading	La lectura / El leer	lek-too-rah / leh-er
Rugby	El rugby	roog-bee
Running	Correr	koh-rrer
Sailing	La navegación a vela	nah-beh-gah-thee-on-ah-beh-lah
Scuba diving	El buceo	boo-theh-oh
Skiing	El esquí	es-kee
Snowboarding	El snowboard	es-noh-bord
Sometimes	A veces	ah-beh-thehs
Sometimes I play chess	A veces juego al ajedrez	ah-beh-thehs-hweh-goh-al-ah-heh-drehth
Sports	Los deportes	deh-por-tehs
Swimming	La natación	nah-tah-thee-on
Tennis	El tenis	teh-nees
Walking	Ambulante	am-boo-lan-teh
Walking	Caminando	kah-mee-nan-doh
Wresting	Lucha	loo-chah
They like	Les gusta	lehs-goos-tah
To box / box	Boxear	bok-seh-ar

Learn Spanish In One Week

English	Spanish	Pronunciation
To cook / cook	Cocinar	koh-thee-nar
To dance / dance	Bailar	beye-lar
To draw / draw	Dibujar	dee-boo-har
To do crosswords	Hacer crucigramas	ah-ther-kroo-thee-grah-mass
To exercise / exercise	Hacer ejercicio	ah-ther-eh-her-thee-thee-oh
To go out with my friends	Salir con mis amigos	sah-leer-kon-mees-ah-mee-gohs
To go shopping	Ir de compras	eer-deh-kom-pras
To go to the cinema	Ir al cine	eer-al-thee-neh
To knit	Tejer	teh-her
To listen to music	Escuchar música	es-koo-char-moo-see-kah
To paint / paint	Pintar	peen-tar
To play cards	Jugar a las cartas	hoo-gar-ah-las-kar-tass
To play the guitar	Tocar la guitarra	toh-kar-lah-gee-tah-rah
To play video games	Jugar videojuegos	hoo-gar-bee-deh-oh-hweh-gos
To read	Leer	leh-er
To ride a bicycle	Montar en bicicleta	mon-tar-en-bee-thee-kleh-tah
To run / run	Correr	koh-rer
To sew	Coser	koh-ser
To sing / sing	Cantar	kan-tar

Learn Spanish In One Week

English	Spanish	Pronunciation
To ski	Esquiar	es-kee-ar
Ski / skiing	esquí	es-kee
To surf the internet	Navegar por internet	nah-beh-gar-por-een-ter-net
To swim / swim	Nadar	nah-dar
Swimming	Natación / nadando	na-tah-thee-on / nah-dan-doh
To talk on the telephone	Hablar por teléfono	ah-blar-por-teh-leh-foh-noh
To travel	Viajar	bee-ah-har
To watch tv	Ver la tele	ber-lah-teh-leh
To write	Escribir	es-kree-beer
To watch television	Mirar la televisión	mee-rar-lah-teh-leh-bee-thee-on
Video games	El videojuego	bee-deh-oh-hweh-goh
Swimming is my favourite sport	La natación es mi deporte favorito	lah-nah-tah-thee-on-es-mee-deh-por-teh-fah-boh-ree-toh
We like	Nos gusta	noss-goos-tah
What do you do in your free time?	¿Qué haces en tu tiempo libre?	keh-ah-thehs-en-too-tee-em-poh-lee-breh
What is your favourite hobby?	¿Cuál es tu pasatiempo favorito?	kwal-es-too-pah-sah-tee-em-poh-fah-boh-ree-toh
Yoga	Yoga	yoh-gah
You like	Te gusta	teh-goos-tah
You like everything	Te gusta todo	teh-goos-tah-toh-doh

Learn Spanish In One Week

Holiday

English	Spanish	Pronunciation
Air-conditioning	El aire acondicionado	eye-reh-ah-kon-dee-thee-oh-nah-doh
Backpack	La mochila	moh-chee-lah
Bucket	El cubo	koo-boh
Caravan	La caravana	kah-rah-bah-nah
City	La ciudad	thee-yoo-dad
First floor	Primer piso	pree-mer-pee-soh
Full board	La pensión completa	pen-see-on-kom-pleh-tah
Half board	La media pensión	meh-dee-ah-pen-see-on
Hotel	El hotel	oh-tell
Ice cream	El helado	eh-lah-doh
Ice rink	La pista de patinaje	pees-tah-deh-pah-teen-ah-heh
I'm going on a cruise	Voy en un crucero	boy-en-oon-kroo-theh-roh
I need a holiday	Necesito unas vacaciones	neh-theh-see-toh-oo-nass-bah-kah-thee-on-ehs
I want to go on holiday	Quiero ir de vacaciones	kee-eh-roh-eer-deh-bah-kah-thee-on-ehs
Indoor swimming pool	La piscina cubierta	pees-thee-nah-koo-bee-er-tah
Journey	El viaje	bee-ah-heh
Key	La llave	yah-beh
Let's go to the beach	Vamos a la playa	bah-moss-ah-lah-plah-yah
Love	El amor	ah-mor

Learn Spanish In One Week

English	Spanish	Pronunciation
Luggage	El equipaje	eh-kee-pah-heh
Map	El mapa	mah-pah
Money	El dinero	dee-neh-roh
Passport	El passaporte	pah-sah-por-teh
Plane	El avión	ah-bee-on
Restaurant	El restaurante	ress-tow-ran-teh
Souvenir	El recuerdo	rreh-kwer-doh
Spade	La pala	pah-lah
Suitcase	La maleta	mah-leh-tah
Swimming pool	La piscina	pees-thee-nah
Taxi	El taxi	tak-see
To rent	Alquilar	al-kee-lar
Tour	El recorrido	rreh-koh-rree-doh
Tourist	El / La turista	too-rees-tah
Where are you going on holiday?	¿A dónde te vas de vacaciones?	ah-don-deh-teh-bass-deh-bah-kah-thee-on-ehs
Where's the swimming pool?	¿Dónde está la piscina?	don-deh-es-tah-lah-pees-thee-nah
What do you do in the summer?	¿Qué haces en verano?	keh-ah-thehs-en-beh-rah-noh
Youth hostel	El albergue juvenil	al-ber-geh-hoo-beh-neel

Learn Spanish In One Week

Hospital & Doctors

English	Spanish	Pronunciation
Abscess	El absceso	abs-theh-soh
Accident	El accidente	ak-thee-den-teh
Allergy	La alergia	ah-ler-hee-ah
Ambulance	La ambulancia	am-boo-lan-thee-ah
Anesthesia	Anestesia	ah-ness-teh-see-ah
Antibiotic	El antibiótico	an-tee-bee-oh-tee-koh
Anxiety	La ansiedad	an-see-eh-dad
Appointment	La cita	thee-tah
Are you hurt?	¿Está herido? / ¿Está herida?	es-tah-er-ee-doh / es-tah-er-ee-dah
Are you sick?	¿Estás enfermo?	es-tass-en-fer-moh
Are you pregnant?	¿Está embarazada?	es-tah-em-bah-rah-thah-dah
Arthritis	La artritis	ar-tree-tees
Asthma	El asma	ass-mah
Backache	El dolor de espalda	doh-lor-deh-es-pal-dah
Bandage	El vendaje	ben-dah-heh
Bed	La cama	kah-mah
Bed pan	El orinal	or-ee-nal
Bee string	La picadura de abeja	pee-kah-doo-rah-deh-ah-beh-hah
Blood	La sangre	san-greh
Blood transfusion	La transfusión de sangre	trans-foo-see-on-deh-san-greh

Learn Spanish In One Week

English	Spanish	Pronunciation
Bone	El hueso	weh-soh
Breathe deeply	Respirar profundo	rress-pee-rah-proh-foon-doh
Breathe deeply	Respirar profundamente	rress-pee-rah-proh-foon-dah-men-teh
Broken bone	El hueso roto	weh-soh-roh-toh
Bruise	El moretón	moh-reh-ton
Burn	La quemadura	keh-mah-doo-rah
Call an ambulance	Llame a una ambulancia	yah-meh-ah-oo-nah-am-boo-lan-thee-ah
Cancer	El cáncer	kan-ther
Can you breathe well?	¿Puede respirar bien?	pweh-deh-res-pee-rar-bee-en
Can you hear?	¿Puedes oír ?	pweh-dehs-oh-eer
Can you move?	¿Puedes moverte / moverse ?	pweh-dehs-moh-ber-teh / moh-ber-seh
Can you move your arm?	¿Puede mover el brazo?	pweh-deh-moh-ber-el-brah-thoh
Can you see?	¿Puedes ver ?	pweh-dehs-ber
Capsule	La cápsula	kap-soo-lah
Cast	El yeso	yeh-soh
Chickenpox	La varicela	bah-ree-theh-lah
Clinic	La clínica	klee-nee-kah
Constipation	El estreñimiento	es-treh-nyee-mee-en-toh

Learn Spanish In One Week

English	Spanish	Pronunciation
Cough	La tos	toss
Cough please	Tos por favor	toss-por-fah-bor
Cramp	El calambre	kah-lam-breh
Cream	La crema	kreh-mah
Crutches	Las muletas	moo-leh-tas
Cut	Corte	kor-teh
Dead	Muerto/a	mwer-toh / tah
Deep pain	El dolor profundo	doh-lor-proh-foon-doh
Dehydration	La deshidratación	des-ee-drah-tah-thee-on
Depression	La depresión	deh-preh-see-on
Diabetes	La diabetes	dee-ah-beh-tehs
Diagnosis	Diagnosis	dee-ag-noh-sees
Diarrhoea	La diarrea	dee-ah-rreh-ah
Diphtheria	La difteria	deef-teh-ree-ah
Dizziness	El mareo	mah-reh-oh
Do you drink?	¿Bebe / Bebes?	beh-beh / beh-behs
Do you have a sore throat?	¿Tienes dolor de garganta?	tee-en-ehs-doh-lor-deh-gar-gan-tah
Do you have any allergies?	¿Tienes alguna alergia?	tee-en-ehs-al-goo-nah-ah-ler-hee-ah
Do you have pain?	¿Tienes dolor?	tee-en-ehs-doh-lor

Learn Spanish In One Week

English	Spanish	Pronunciation
Do you smoke?	¿Fuma / Fumas?	foo-mah / foo-mass
Do you take any medicine?	¿Toma algún medicamento?	toh-mah-al-goon-meh-dee-kah-men-toh
Doctor	El doctor / La doctora	dok-tor / dok-toh-rah
Doctor	El médico / La médica	meh-dee-koh / meh-dee-kah
Does it hurt?	¿Te duele / Le duele?	teh-dweh-leh / leh-dweh-leh
Does that hurt?	¿Eso duele?	eh-soh-dweh-leh
Does this hurt?	¿Duele esto?	dweh-leh-es-toh
Does this hurt?	¿Esto duele?	es-toh-dweh-leh
Drip	El suero	sweh-roh
Drops	Las gotas	goh-tas
Dry eye	El ojo seco	oh-hoh-seh-koh
Dry mouth	La boca seca	boh-kah-seh-kah
Dysentery	La disenteria	dee-sen-teh-ree-ah
Ear ache	El dolor de oído	doh-lor-deh-oh-ee-doh
Emergency room	La sala de emergencia	sah-lah-deh-eh-mer-hen-thee-ah
Entrance	La entrada	en-trah-dah
Examination	El reconocimiento	rreh-koh-noh-thee-mee-en-toh
Exit	La salida	sah-lee-dah
Fever	La fiebre	fee-eh-breh

Learn Spanish In One Week

English	Spanish	Pronunciation
Food poisoning	La intoxicación alimentaria	een-tok-see-kah-thee-on-ah-lee-men-tah-ree-ah
Fracture	La fractura	frak-too-rah
German measles	La rubeola	rroo-beh-oh-lah
Have you felt dizzy?	¿Se ha sentido mareado?	seh-hah-sen-tee-doh-mah-reh-ah-doh
Heart attack	Un ataque al corazón	ah-tah-keh-al-koh-rah-thon
Heart attack	Un ataque cardíaco	ah-tah-keh-kar-dee-ah-koh
Heart attack	El infarto	een-far-toh
Heartburn	La acidez	ah-thee-deth
High blood pressure	La presión alta	preh-see-on-al-tah
High cholesterol	Colesterol alto	kol-es-teh-rol-al-toh
Hospital	El hospital	os-pee-tal
How can I help you?	¿Cómo puedo ayudarte?	koh-moh-pweh-doh-ah-yoo-dar-teh
How do you feel?	¿Cómo te sientes?	koh-moh-teh-see-en-tehs
How is your appetite?	¿Cómo es tu apetito?	koh-moh-es-too-ah-peh-tee-toh
I'm allergic to cats	Soy alérgico a los gatos	soy-ah-ler-hee-koh-ah-loss-gah-toss
I'm allergic to dairy	Soy alérgico a los productos lácteos	soy-ah-ler-hee-koh-ah-loss-proh-dook-toss-lak-teh-oss

Learn Spanish In One Week

English	Spanish	Pronunciation
I'm allergic to nuts	Soy alérgico a los frutos secos	soy-ah-ler-hee-koh-ah-loss-froo-toss-seh-koss
I'm allergic to nuts	Soy alérgico a las nueces	soy-ah-ler-hee-koh-ah-lass-noo-eh-thehs
I'm allergic to penicillin	Soy alérgico a la penicilina	soy-ah-ler-hee-koh-ah-la-peh-nee-thee-lee-nah
I'm diabetic	Soy diabético	soy-dee-ah-beh-tee-koh
I'm going to listen to your heart	Voy a escuchar a su corazón	boy-ah-es-koo-char-ah-soo-coh-rah-thon
I am hot	Tengo calor	ten-goh-kah-lor
I am ill	Estoy enfermo	es-toy-en-fer-moh
I'm on the pill	Estoy en la píldora	es-toy-en-lah-peel-doh-rah
I'm on the pill	Tomo la píldora	toh-moh-lah-peel-doh-rah
I'm pregnant	Estoy embarazada	es-toy-em-bah-rah-thah-dah
I am sweating	Estoy sudando	es-toy-soo-dan-doh
I can't	No puedo	noh-pweh-doh
I can't breathe	No puedo respirar	noh-pweh-doh-rehs-pee-rar
I can't eat	No puede comer	noh-pweh-doh-koh-mer
I can't sleep	No puedo dormir	noh-pweh-doh-dor-meer
I don't feel well	No me siento bien	noh-meh-see-en-toh-bee-en
I feel dizzy	Me siento mareado	meh-see-en-toh-mah-reh-ah-doh
I feel sick	Estoy mareando	es-toy-mah-reh-an-doh

Learn Spanish In One Week

English	Spanish	Pronunciation
I feel sick	No me siento bien	noh-meh-see-en-toh-bee-en
I feel tired	Me siento cansado	meh-see-en-toh-kan-sah-doh
I have	Tengo	ten-goh
I have a bite	Tengo una picadura	ten-goh-oo-nah-pee-kah-doo-rah
I have a cold	Tengo un catarro	ten-goh-oon-kah-tah-rroh
I have a cold	Tengo un resfriado	ten-goh-oon-res-free-ah-doh
I have a cough	Tengo tos	ten-goh-toss
I have a cut on my leg	Tengo un corte en mi pierna	ten-goh-oon-kor-teh-en-mee-pee-er-nah
I have a fever	Tengo fiebre	ten-goh-fee-eh-breh
I have a headache	Me duele la cabeza	meh-dwel-eh-lah-kah-beh-thah
I have a headache	Tengo dolor de cabeza	ten-goh-doh-lor-deh-kah-beh-thah
I have an appointment	Tengo una cita	ten-goh-oo-nah-thee-tah
I have stomach ache	Tengo dolor de estómago	ten-goh-doh-lor-deh-es-toh-mah-goh
I have chest pain / My chest hurts	Me duele el pecho	meh-dwel-eh-el-peh-choh
I have heat stroke	Tengo insolación	ten-goh-een-soh-lah-thee-on
I have shivers	Tengo escalofríos	ten-goh-es-kal-oh-free-ohs
I have the flu	Tengo gripe	ten-goh-gree-peh
I need help	Necesito ayuda	neh-theh-see-toh-ah-yoo-dah

Learn Spanish In One Week

English	Spanish	Pronunciation
I need to see a doctor	Necesito ver un médico	neh-theh-see-toh-ber-oon-meh-dee-koh
Infection	La infección	een-fek-thee-on
Injury	La herida	eh-ree-dah
Insomnia	El insomnio	een-som-nee-oh
Insurance	El seguro	seh-goo-roh
Insurance forms	Formularios de seguro	for-moo-lah-ree-oss-seh-goo-roh
Itching	La picazón	pee-kah-thon
I think I'm going to throw up	Creo que voy a vomitar	kreh-oh-keh-boy-ah-bom-ee-tar
It hurts	Me duele	meh-dwel-eh
It hurts a lot	Duele mucho	dweh-leh-moo-choh
It hurts here	Duele aquí	dweh-leh-ah-kee
It hurts there	Duele allí	dweh-leh-ah-yee
It's not serious	No es grave	noh-es-grah-beh
It is very serious	Es muy grave	es-mwee-grah-beh
I want to throw up	Quiero vomitar	kee-eh-roh-bom-ee-tar
Lie down	Acostarse	ah-koss-tar-seh
Lie down please	Acuéstese por favor	ah-kweh-steh-seh-por-fah-bor
Low blood pressure	La presión baja	preh-see-on-bah-hah
Malaria	La malaria	mah-lah-ree-ah

Learn Spanish In One Week

English	Spanish	Pronunciation
Mask	La mascarilla	mass-kah-ree-yah
Measles	La sarampión	sah-ram-pee-on
Medicine	La medicina	meh-dee-thee-nah
Migraine	La migraña	mee-grah-nyah
Miscarriage	El aborto espontáneo	ah-bor-toh-es-pon-tah-nee-oh
Mumps	Las paperas	pah-peh-ras
My back hurts	Me duele la espalda	meh-dweh-leh-lah-es-pal-dah
Needle	La aguja	ah-goo-hah
No I don't have	No no tengo	noh-noh-ten-goh
No my throat doesn't hurt	No me duele la garganta	noh-meh-dweh-leh-lah-gar-gan-tah
Nurse	El enfermero / era	en-fer-meh-roh / rah
Open your mouth	Abra la boca / Abre la boca	ah-brah-lah-boh-kah / ah-breh-lah-boh-kah
Pain	El dolor	doh-lor
Painkiller	El analgésico	an-al-hess-ee-koh
Panic attack	El ataque de pánico	ah-tah-keh-deh-pah-nee-koh
Patient	El / La paciente	pah-thee-en-teh
Pharmacy	La farmacia	far-mah-thee-ah
Pill	La pastilla	pass-tee-yah

Learn Spanish In One Week

English	Spanish	Pronunciation
Please take this medicine	Por favor tome esta medicina	por-fah-bor-toh-meh-es-tah-meh-dee-thee-nah
Pneumonia	La neumonía	neh-oo-moh-nee-ah
Point to where it hurts	Señale dónde le duele	sen-yah-leh-don-deh-leh-dweh-leh
Poisoning	La envenenamiento	en-beh-neh-nah-mee-en-toh
Poor appetite	La falta de apetito	fal-tah-deh-ah-peh-tee-toh
Prescription	La receta	reh-theh-tah
Pregnant	Embarazada	em-bah-rah-thah-dah
Rabies	La rabia	rah-bee-ah
Rash	La erupción	eh-roop-thee-on
Rash	La sarpullido	sar-poo-yee-doh
Scalpel	El bisturí	bees-too-ree
Seizure	Convulsión	kon-bul-see-on
Sensitive	Sensible	sen-see-bleh
Shortness of breath	Falta de aliento	fal-tah-deh-ah-lee-en-toh
Since last week	Desde la semana pasada	dehs-deh-la-seh-mah-nah-pah-sah-dah
Since Tuesday	Desde el martes	dehs-deh-el-mar-tehs
Since yesterday	Desde ayer	dehs-deh-ah-yer
Sometimes	A verces	ah-beh-thehs

Learn Spanish In One Week

English	Spanish	Pronunciation
Sore throat	El dolor de garganta	doh-lor-deh-gar-gan-tah
Sprain	El esguince	es-geen-theh
Sting	La picadura	pee-kah-doo-rah
Stress	El estrés	es-tress
Stuffy nose	Nariz tapada	nah-reeth-tah-pah-dah
Sunburn	La quemadura de sol	keh-mah-doo-rah-deh-sol
Sunstroke	La insolación	een-soh-lah-thee-on
Surgeon	El cirujano / La cirujana	thee-roo-hah-noh / thee roo-hah-nah
Surgery	La cirguía	thee-roo-hee-ah
Swollen	Hinchado	een-chah-doh
Syringe	La jeringa	heh-reen-gah
Tablet	La pastilla	pass-tee-yah
Take a deep breathe	Respira profundo	res-pee-rah-proh-foon-doh
To cough	Toser	toh-ser
Tonsillitis	La amigdalitis	ah-meeg-dah-lee-tees
Transplant	El transplante / trasplante	trans-plan-teh / tras-plan-teh
Trauma	Trauma	trow-mah
Treatment	El tratamiento	trah-tah-mee-en-toh
Typhoid	La tifoidea	tee-foy-deh-ah
Ulcer	La úlcera	ool-theh-rah

Learn Spanish In One Week

English	Spanish	Pronunciation
Upset stomach	El malestrar de estómago	mal-eh-strar-deh-es-toh-mah-goh
Urgent	Urgente	oor-hen-teh
Urine sample	La muestra de orina	moo-es-trah-deh-or-ee-nah
Vaccination	La vacunación	bah-koo-nah-thee-on
Vaccine	La vacuna	bah-koo-nah
Virus	Virus	bee-roos
Visitor	La visita	bee-see-tah
Vomit	El vómito	boh-mee-toh
Ward	La sala	sah-lah
Wart	La verruga	beh-rroo-gah
Weight loss	La pédida de peso	per-dee-dah-deh-peh-soh
What can I do you you?	¿Qué puedo hacer por usted?	keh-pweh-doh-ah-ther-por-oo-sted
What happened?	¿Qué pasó?	keh-pah-soh
What's the matter?	¿Qué pasa?	keh-pah-sah
Where's the doctor?	¿Dónde está el médico?	don-deh-es-tah-el-meh-dee-koh
What's the problem?	¿Cuál es el problema?	kwal-es-el-proh-bleh-mah
Where does it hurt?	Dónde te duele	don-deh-teh-dweh-leh
Wound	La herida	eh-ree-dah

Learn Spanish In One Week

Hotel

English	Spanish	Pronunciation
Air conditioning	El aire acondicionado	eye-reh-ak-kon-dee-thee-oh-nah-doh
Are there any towels?	¿Hay toallas?	eye-toh-ah-yas
Bathrobe	El albornoz	al-bor-noth
Bellboy	El botones	boh-toh-nehs
Bill	La cuenta	kwen-tah
Blanket	La manta	man-tah
Complaint	Una queja	keh-hah
Complaint	Reclamación	rreh-klah-mah-thee-on
Double bed	Una cama de matrimonial	kah-mah-deh-mah-tree-moh-nee-al
Double bed	Una cama doble	kah-mah-doh-bleh
Double room	Una habitación doble	ah-bee-tah-thee-on-doh-bleh
Do you have?	¿Tiene / Tienes?	tee-en-eh / tee en-ehs
For how many night?	Para cuántas noches	pah-rah-kwan-tass-noh-chehs
Hot water	El agua caliente	ah-gwah-kah-lee-en-teh
How much is the room?	¿Cuánto cuesta la habitación?	kwan-toh-kweh-stah-lah-ah-bee-tah-thee-on
I'd like to make a reservation?	¿Me gustaría hacer una reserva?	meh-goos-tah-ree-ah-ah-ther-oo-nah-reh-ser-bah
Is there any? / Are there any?	¿Hay?	eye

Learn Spanish In One Week

English	Spanish	Pronunciation
Is the room ready?	¿Está lista la habitación?	es-tah-lees-tah-lah-ah-bee-tah-thee-on
Key	La llave	yah-beh
Manager	El director	dee-rek-tor
Reception	La recepción	rreh-thep-thee-on
Receptionist	El / La recepcionista	rreh-thep-thee-oh-nees-tah
Reservation	Una reserva	rreh-ser-bah
Room with a view	Una habitación con vistas	ah-bee-tah-thee-on-kon-bees-tass
Sheets	La sábanas	sah-bah-nass
Single bed	Una cama individual	kah-mah-een-dee-bee-doo-al
Single room	Una habitación individual	ah-bee-tah-thee-on-een-dee-bee-doo-al
Tip	Una propiina	proh-pee-nah
Towel	La toalla	toh-ah-yah
View	Una vista	bees-tah
What kind of room do you need?	¿Qué tipo de habitación necesita?	keh-tee-poh-deh-ah-bee-tah-thee-on-neh-theh-see-tah
What time is breakfast?	¿A qué hora es el desayuno?	ah-keh-oh-rah-es-el-deh-say-oo-noh
Where can I park my car?	¿Dónde puedo aparcar mí coche?	don-deh-pweh-doh-ah-par-kar-mee-koh-cheh
Yes of course here you are	Sí claro aquí tiene	see-klah-roh-ah-kee-tee-eh-neh

Learn Spanish In One Week
House

English	Spanish	Pronunciation
Back door	La puerta trasera	pwer-tah-trah-seh-rah
Banister	La barandilla	bah-ran-dee-yah
Bath / Bathtub	La bañera	ban-yeh-rah
Bathroom	El baño	ban-yoh
Bathroom	El cuarto de baño	kwar-toh-deh-ban-yoh
Bed	La cama	kah-mah
Bedroom	El cuarto	kwar-toh
Bedroom	El dormitorio	dor-mee-toh-ree-oh
Bedroom	La habitación	ah-bee-tah-thee-on
Bedside lamp	La lámpara de mesa	lam-pah-rah-deh-meh-sah
Bedside table	La mesa de noche	meh-sah-deh-noh-cheh
Bedside table	La mesita de noche	meh-see-tah-deh-noh-cheh
Bin / Bucket	El cubo	koo-boh
Bin	La papelera	pah-peh-leh-rah
Blanket	La manta	man-tah
Blinds	La persiana	per-see-ah nah
Blinds for windows	Las persianas para ventanas	per-see-ah-nas-pah-rah-ben-tah-nas
Book	El libro	lee-broh
Bottle opener	El abrebotellas	ah-breh-boh-teh-yahs

Learn Spanish In One Week

English	Spanish	Pronunciation
Bowl	El bol	bol
Bowl	El cuenco	kwen-koh
Bowl	El tazón	tah-thon
Bread bin	La panera	pah-neh-rah
Brick	El ladrillo	lah-dree-yoh
Brush	El cepillo	theh-pee-yoh
Bucket	El cubo	koo-boh
Carpet	La alfombra	al fom-brah
Carpet	La moqueta	moh-keh-tah
Ceiling	El techo	teh-choh
Central heating	La calefacción central	kah-leh-fak-thee-on-th-en-tral
Chair	La silla	see-yah
Chimney	La chimenea	chee-meh-neh-ah
Clothes line	El tendedero	ten-deh-deh-roh
Clock	El reloj	reh-loh
Coat hanger	La percha	per-chah
Coffee table	La mesa de centro	meh-sah-deh-th-en-troh
Cold water	El agua fría	ah-gwah-free-ah
Computer	El ordenador	or-deh-nah-dor
Cooker / Stove	La cocina	koh-thee-nah

Learn Spanish In One Week

English	Spanish	Pronunciation
Couch	El sofá	soh-fah
Cup	La taza	tah-thah
Cupboard	La alacena	ah-lah-theh-nah
Cupboard / drawer	La gaveta	gah-beh-tah
Cushion	El cojín	koh-heen
Curtain	La cortina	kor-tee-nah
Don't wipe your hands on the tablecloth	No te limpies las manos con el mantel	noh-teh-leem-pee-ehs-las mah-nos-kon-el-man-tel
Door	La puerta	pwer-tah
Doorbell	El timbre	teem-breh
Doorknob	El pomo	poh-moh
Doormat	El felpudo	fel-poo-doh
Downstairs	Abajo	ah-bah-hoh
Downstairs	En el piso de abajo	en-el-pee-soh-deh-ah-bah-hoh
Drain	El desagüe	dehs-ah-gweh
Drawer	El cajón	kah-hon
Fire	El fuego	fweh-goh
Fireplace	La chimenea	chee-meh-neh-ah
First floor	Primer piso	pree-mer-pee-soh
Floor / story	El piso	pee-soh

Learn Spanish In One Week

English	Spanish	Pronunciation
Floor	El suelo	sweh-loh
Fork	El tenedor	teh-neh-dor
Freezer	El congelador	kon-heh-lah-dor
Fridge	La nevera	neh-beh-rah
Front door	La puerta principal	pwer-tah-preen-thee-pal
Frying pan	El / La sartén	sar-ten
Garage	El garaje	gah-rah-heh
Garden	El jardín	har-deen
Garden hose	La manguera	man-geh-rah
Garden wall	La tapia	tah-pee-ah
Glass (with stem)	La copa	koh-pah
Glass	El vaso	bah-soh
Grill	La parrilla	pah-rree-yah
Gutter	El canalón	kah-nah-lon
Hairdryer	El secador de pelo	seh-kah-dor-deh-peh-loh
Headboard	El cabecera	kah-beh-theh-rah
Heating	La calefacción	kah-leh-fak-thee-on
Hair conditioner	El acondicionador de cabello	ah-kon-dee-thee-on-ah-dor-deh-kah-beh-yoh
Home	La casa	kah-sah

Learn Spanish In One Week

English	Spanish	Pronunciation
Hot water	El agua caliente	ah-gwah-kah-lee-en-teh
House	La casa	kah-sah
I'm going home	Voy a casa	boy-ah-kah-sah
Iron	La plancha	plan-char
Ironing board	La tabla de planchar	tah-blah-deh-plan-char
It's upstairs	Está arriba	es-tah-ah-rree-bah
Kettle	El hervidor	er-bee-dor
Key	La llave	yah-beh
Kitchen	La cocina	koh-thee-nah
Knife	El cuchillo	koo-chee-yoh
Letterbox	El buzón	boo-thon
Light	La luz	looth
Light bulb	La bombilla	bom-bee-yah
Light switch	El interruptor	een-teh-rroop-tor
Living room	La sala	sah-lah
Living room	El salón	sah-lon
Mattress	El colchón	kohl-chon
Microwave	El microondas	mee-kroh-on-das
Mirror	El espejo	es-peh-hoh
Mop	La mopa	moh-pah

Learn Spanish In One Week

English	Spanish	Pronunciation
Napkin	La servilleta	ser-bee-yeh-tah
Painting	El cuadro	kwah-droh
Painting	La pintura	peen-too-rah
Picture frame	El marco	mar-koh
Pillow	La almohada	al-moh-ah-dah
Plant	La planta	plan-tah
Plate	El plato	plah-toh
Plug (electric)	El enchufe	en-choo-feh
Plug (bath/sink)	El tapón	tah-pon
Portrait	El retrato	reh-trah-toh
Radiator	El radiador	rrah-dee-ah-dor
Refrigerator	El frigorifico	free-goh-ree-fee-koh
Refrigerator	La nevera	neh-beh-rah
Room	El cuarto	kwar-toh
Room	La habitación	ah-bee-tah-thee-on
Rug	La alfombra	al-fom-brah
Rug	La alfombrilla	al-fom-bree-yah
Saucepan	La cacerola	kah-theh-roh-lah
Scissors	Las tijeras	tee-her-ass
Second floor	Segundo piso	seh-goon-doh-pee-soh

Learn Spanish In One Week

English	Spanish	Pronunciation
Settee	El sofá	soh-fah
Shampoo	El champú	cham-poo
Shaving cream	La crema de afeitar	kreh-mah-deh-ah-feh-tar
Sheet	La sábana	sah-bah-nah
Shelf	El estante	es-tan-teh
Shower	La ducha	doo-chah
Shower cap	El gorro de ducha	goh-roh-deh-doo-chah
Shower curtain	La cortina de ducha	kor-tee-nah-deh-doo-chah
Shower gel	El gel de ducha	hel-deh-doo-chah
Shower head	La alcachofa de la ducha	al-kah-choh-fah-deh-lah-doo-chah
Soap	El jabón	hah-bon
Sofa	El sofá	soh-fah
Spoon	La cuchara	koo-chah-rah
Stairs	Las escaleras	es-kah-leh-ras
Table	La mesa	meh-sah
Tablecloth	El mantel	man-tel
Table lamp	La lámpara de mesa	lam-pah-rah-deh-meh-sah
Tap	El grifo	gree-foh
Teapot	La tetera	teh-teh-rah
Teaspoon	La cucharita	koo-chah-ree-tah

Learn Spanish In One Week

English	Spanish	Pronunciation
Telephone	El teléfono	teh-leh-foh-noh
Television	La televisión	teh-leh-bee-see-on
Tile (floor)	La baldosa	bal-doh-sah
Tile (roof)	La teja	teh-hah
Tile (wall)	El azulejo	ah-thoo-leh-hoh
Tin opener	El abreletas	ah-breh-lah-tas
Third floor	Tercer piso	ter-ther-pee-soh
This is my house	Esta es mi casa	es-tah-es-mee-kah-sah
Toaster	La tostadora	tos-tah-doh-rah
Toilet	El escusado	es-koo-sah-doh
Toilet	El retrete	rreh-treh-teh
Toilet	El váter	bah-ter
Toilets (room)	El aseo	ah-seh-oh
Toilets (room) / bath	El baño	ban-yoh
Toilet (room) / sink	El lavabo	lah-bah-boh
Toilet (room)	El servicio	ser-bee-thee-oh
Toilet brush	La escobilla	es-koh-bee-yah
Toilet paper	El papel higiénico	pah-pel-ee-hen-ee-koh
Toilet plunger	El desatascador	deh-sah-tas-kah-dor
Toilet plunger	El destapador	des-tah-pah-dor

Learn Spanish In One Week

English	Spanish	Pronunciation
Toilet seat	El asiento del inodoro	ah-see-en-toh-del-een-oh-doh-roh
Toilet seat	El asiento del váter	ah-see-en-toh-del-bah-ter
Tooth brush	El cepillo de dientes	theh-pee-yoh-deh-dee-en-tehs
Tooth paste	La pasta de dientes	pas-tah-deh-dee-en-tehs
Towel	La toalla	toh-ah-yah
Upstairs	Arriba	ah-rree-bah
Upstairs	El piso de arriba	el-pee-soh-deh-ah-rree-bah
Vacuum cleaner	La aspiradora	ass-pee-rah-doh-rah
Wall	El muro	moo-roh
Wall (inside)	La pared	pah-red
Wallpaper	El papel pintado	pah-pel-peen-tah-doh
Wardrobe	El armario	ahr-mah-ree-oh
Washbasin	El lavabo	lah-bah-boh
Washing machine	La lavadora	lah-bah-doh-rah
Washing powder	El jabón en polvo	hah-bon-en-pol-boh
Washing-up liquid	El lavavajillas	lah-bah-bah-hee-yahs
Watch	El reloj	rreh-loh
Watering can	La regadera	reh-gah-deh-rah
Window	La ventana	ben-tah-nah

Learn Spanish In One Week

Human Beings

English	Spanish	Pronunciation
Adolescent	Adolescente	ah-doh-lehs-th-en-teh
Adult	El adulto	ah-dool-toh
Baby	El / La bebé	beh-beh
Beggar	El mendigo	men-dee-goh
Best friend	El / La mejor amigo/a	meh-hor-ah-mee-goh / gah
Boss	El jefe / La jefa	heh-feh / heh-fah
Boss	El patrón / La patrona	pah-tron / pah-troh-nah
Boy	El chico	chee-koh
Boy	El niño	nee-nyoh
Boyfriend	El novio	noh-bee-oh
Child	El niño / La niña	nee-nyoh / nee-nyah
Children	Los niños / Las niñas	neen-yoss / neen-yass
Fan (pop / sport)	El / La fan	fan
Foreigner	El extranjero	eks-tran-heh-roh
Friend	El amigo / La amiga	ah-mee-goh / ah-mee-gah
Gang	La banda	ban-dah
Girl	La chica	chee-kah
Girl	La niña	nee-nyah
Girlfriend	La novia	noh-bee-ah
Holidaymaker	El / La veraneante	beh-ran-neh-an-teh

Learn Spanish In One Week

English	Spanish	Pronunciation
Hooligan	El / La hooligan	oo-lee-gan
Manager	El / La encargado / da	en-kar-gah-doh / dah
Manager	El / La director / a	dee-rek-tor / dee rek toh-rah
Manager	El / La gerente	heh-ren-teh
Neighbour	El vecino	beh-thee-noh
Old person	El anciano / La anciana	an-thee-ah-noh / an-thee-an-ah
Passenger	El pasajero	pah-sah-heh-roh
Pensioner / OAP	El jubilado	hoo-bee-lah-doh
People	Gente	hen-teh
Stranger	Extraño	eks-trah-nyoh
Student	El / La estudiante	es-too-dee-an-teh
Teenager	Adolescente	ah-doh-lehs-th-en-teh
Terrorist	El / La terrorista	teh-rroh-rees-tah
Tourist	El turisto / La turista	too-rees-toh / too-rees-tah
Tourist	Turístico	too-rees-tee-koh
Tramp	El / La vagabundo / da	bah-gah-boon-doh / dah
Woman	La mujer	moo-her
Woman	La señora	seh-nyoh-rah
Young man	El joven	hoh-ben
Young woman	La joven	hoh-ben

Learn Spanish In One Week

Leisure / Date Ideas

English	Spanish	Pronunciation
Go bowling	Ir a jugar a los bolos	eer-ah-hoo-gar-ah-los-boh-los
Go camping	Ir a campar	eer-ah-kam-par
Go dancing	Ir a bailar	eer-ah-beye-lar
Go horse riding	Ir a caballo	eer-ah-kah-bah-yoh
Go skating	Ir a patinar	eer-ah-pah-tee-nar
Go swimming	Ir a nadar	eer-ah-nah-dar
Go for a drive	Dar un paseo	dar-oon-pah-seh-oh
Go for a walk	Dar un paseo	dar-oon-pah-seh-oh
Go on holiday	Ir de vacaciones	eer-deh-bah-kah-thee-on-ehs
Go shopping	Ir de compras	eer-deh-kom-pras
Go to a concert	Ir a un concierto	eer-ah-oon-kon-thee-er-toh
Go for a bicycle ride	Dar un paseo en bicicleta	dar-oon-pah-seh-oh-en-bee-thee-kleh-tah
Go to a museum	Ir a un museo	eer-ah-oon-moo-seh-oh
Go to a party	Ir a una fiesta	eer-ah-oo-nah-fee-es-tah
Go for a picnic	Ir de picnic	eer-deh-peek-neek
Go to a restaurant	Ir a un restaurante	eer-ah-oon-rres-tow-ran-teh
Go to the cinema	Ir al cine	eer-al-thee-neh
Go to the theatre	Ir al teatro	eer-al-teh-ah-troh
Go to the zoo	Ir al zoológico	eer-al-thoh-loh-hee-koh

Learn Spanish In One Week

Love

English	Spanish	Pronunciation
Affection	Cariño	kah-ree-nyoh
Are you married?	¿Estás casado / da?	es-tas-kah-sah-doh- / dah
Are you single?	¿Estás soltero / ra?	es-tas-sol-teh-roh / rah
Baby	Bebé	beh-beh
Cuddle / hug	Abrazo	ah-brah-thoh
Cutie	Cosita	koh-see-tah
Date	Cita	thee-tah
Darling	Cariño	kah-ree-nyoh
Do you love me?	¿Ma amas?	meh-ah-mass
Fatty	Gordito	gor-dee-toh
Happiness	La felicidad	feh-lee-thee-dad
I'm in love	Estoy enamorado	es-toy-eh-nah-moh-rah-doh
I'm in love with you	Estoy enamorado de ti	es-toy-eh-nah-moh-rah-doh-deh-tee
I'm married	Soy casado / da	soy-kah-sah-doh / dah
I'm single	Soy soltero	soy-sol-teh-roh
I also love you	También te quiero	tam-bee-en-teh-kee-eh-roh
I can't live without you	No puedo vivir sin ti	noh-pweh-doh-bee-beer-seen-tee
I don't feel the same	No siento lo mismo	noh-see-en-toh-loh-mees-moh
I don't love you	No te amo	noh-teh-ah-moh
I don't love you	Yo no te quiero	yoh-noh-teh-kee-eh-roh

Learn Spanish In One Week

English	Spanish	Pronunciation
I like you	Me gustas	meh-goos-tas
I love you	Te amo	teh-ah-moh
I love you more each day	Te amo más cada día	teh-ah-moh-mass-kah-dah-dee-ah
I love you too	Te quiero también	teh-kee-eh-roh-tam-bee-en
I love you too	También te amo	tam-bee-en-teh-ah-moh
I love you too	Yo también te amo	yoh-tam-bee-en-teh-ah-moh
I miss you	Te extraño	teh-eks-trah-nyoh
I need you	Te necesito	teh-neh-thee-see-toh
In love	Enamorado	eh-nah-moh-rah-doh
I want another drink	Quiero otra bebida	kee-eh-roh-oh-trah-beh-bee-dah
I want another ice-cream	Quiero otro helado	kee-eh-roh-oh-troh-el-ah-doh
I want you / I love you	Te quiero	teh-kee-eh-roh
Kiss	El beso	beh-soh
Let's be friends	Seamos amigos	seh-ah-moss-ah-mee-gohs
Love	El amor	ah-mor
Lover	El / La amante	ah-man-teh
Marriage	Matrimonio	mah-tree-moh-nee-oh
Married	Casado	kah-sah-doh
Me too	Yo también	yoh-tam-bee-en
My boyfriend	Mi novio	mee-noh-bee-oh

Learn Spanish In One Week

English	Spanish	Pronunciation
My fiancé	Mi prometido	mee-prom-eh-tee-doh
My fiancée	Mi prometida	mee-prom-eh-tee-dah
My girlfriend	Mi novia	mee-noh-bee-ah
My heaven	Mi cielo	mee-thee-eh-loh
My husband	Mi esposo	mee-es-poh-soh
My king	Mi rey	mee-reh
My life	Mi vida	mee-bee-dah
My love	Mi amor	mee-ah-mor
My queen	Mi reina	mee-reh-nah
My treasure	Me tesoro	mee-teh-soh-roh
My wife	Mi esposa	mee-es-poh-sah
Romantic partner	Mi compañero / ra	mee-kom-pan-yeh-roh / rah
Single	Soltero	sol-teh-roh
Sorry but I don't like you	Perdon pero no me gustas	per-don-peh-roh-noh-meh-goos-tas
Sorry but I don't love you	Lo siento pero no te amo	loh-see-en-toh-peh-roh-noh-teh-ah-moh
Sweetheart	Corazón	koh-rah-thon
Thingy	Cosita	koh-see-tah
To fall in love	Enamorarse	eh-nah-moh-rah-seh
We're dating	Estamos saliendo	es-tah-moss-sah-lee-en-doh

Learn Spanish In One Week

English	Spanish	Pronunciation
We're going out	Estamos saliendo	es-tah-moss-sah-lee-en-doh
We are engaged	Estamos comprometidos	es-tah-moss-kom-prom-eh-tee-dohs
We got engaged	Nos comprometimos	noss-kom-prom-eh-tee-moss
We got married	Nos casamos	noss-kah-sah-moss
We got married last year	Nos casamos el año pasado	noss-kah-sah-moss-el-an-yoh-pah-sah-doh
Wedding	La boda	boh-dah
Wedding	El casamiento	kah-sah-mee-en-toh
Wedding cake	El pastel de boda	pah-stel-deh-boh-dah
Wedding dress	El vestido ve novia	bes-tee-boh-deh-noh-bee-ah
Wedding ring	El anillo de casado	an-ee-yoh-deh-kah-sah-doh
You are a wonderful person	Eres una persona maravillosa	eh-rehs-oo-nah-per-soh-nah-mah-rah-bee-yoh-sah
You are beautiful	Eres hermoso/a	eh-rehs-er-moh-soh / sah
You are everything to me	Eres todo para mí	eh-rehs-toh-doh-pah-rah-mee
You are my everything	Eres mi todo	eh-rehs-mee-toh-doh
You are so beautiful	Eres muy hermoso/a	eh-rehs-mwee-er-moh-soh / sah
You drive me crazy	Me vuelves loco/a	meh-bwel-behs-loh-koh / kah
You mean so much to me	Significas mucho para mí	seeg-nee-fee-kass-moo-choh-pah-rah-mee

Learn Spanish In One Week

Market - shopping - Supermarket

English	Spanish	Pronunciation
Affordable	Económico/a	eh-koh-noh-mee-koh / kah
Are credit cards accepted?	¿Se aceptan tarjeta de crédito?	seh-ah-thep-tan-tar-heh-tah-deh-kreh-dee-toh
Are there any cold beers?	¿Hay cervezas frías?	eye-th-er-beh-thass-free-ass
Cashier	Cajero/a	kah-heh-roh / rah
Cash register	La caja	kah-hah
Change	Cambio	kam-bee-oh
Cheap	Barato/a	bah-rah-toh / tah
Closed	Cerrado	theh-rrah-doh
Credit card	La tarjeta de crédito	tar-heh-tah-deh-kreh-dee-toh
Dairy	Lácteos	lak-teh-ohs
Day of the Dead	El Día de los Muertos	el-dee-ah-deh-los-mwer-toss
Delicious	Delicioso/a	deh-lee-thee-oh-soh / sah
Discount	Descuento	des-kwen-toh
Electronics	Electrónica	eh-lek-troh-nee-kah
Entrance	Entrada	en-trah-dah
Exit	Salida	sah-lee-dah
Expensive	Caro/a	kah-roh /rah
For sale	A la venta	ah-lah-ben-tah
For sale	En venta	en-ben-tah

Learn Spanish In One Week

English	Spanish	Pronunciation
Fruit and Vegetables	Frutas y verduras	froo-tas-ee-ber-doo-ras
Gardening	Jardinería	har-dee-neh-ree-ah
Good quality	Buena calidad	bweh-nah-kah-lee-dad
Here's your change	Aquí está su cambio	ah-kee-es-tah-soo-kam-bee-oh
Holiday/Party/Day Off	La fiesta	fee-es-tah
I'm coming back soon	Vuelvo pronto	bwel-boh-pron-toh
I'm just looking	Sólo estoy mirando	soh-loh-es-toy-mee-ran-doh
I'm just looking	Sólo quería mirar	soh-loh-keh-ree-ah-mee-rar
I don't want it	No lo quiero	noh-loh-kee-eh-roh
I'd like to try it on	Quisiera probarlo	kee-see-eh-rah-proh-bar-loh
Is there?	¿Hay?	eye
I want	Quiero	kee-eh-roh
I'll come back later	Vuelvo más tarde	bwel-boh-mas-tar-deh
I'll come back soon	Volveré pronto	bol-beh-reh-pron-toh
I'll think about it	Voy a pensarlo	boy-ah-pen-sar-loh
In other colours	En otros colores	en-oh-trohs-kol-or-ehs
In other sizes	En otras tallas	en-oh-tras-tal-yahs
Large	Grande	gran-deh
Luxurious	Lujoso	loo-hoh-soh
Meats	Carnes	kar-nehs

Learn Spanish In One Week

English	Spanish	Pronunciation
Medium	Mediano/a	meh-dee-ah-noh / nah
On sale	En oferta	en-oh-fer-tah
Open	Abierto	ah-bee-er-toh
Open at ten	Abierto a las diez	ah-bee-er-toh-ah-las-dee-eth
Poor quality	Mala calidad	mah-lah-kah-lee-dad
Pull	Jale	hah-leh
Push	Empujar	em-poo-har
Receipt	El recibo	rreh-thee-boh
Reduced / Discount	De rebaja	deh-rreh-bah-hah
Reduced / Discount	Rebaja	rreh-bah-hah
Seller	Vendedor	ben-deh-dor
Small	Pequeño/a	peh-keh-nyoh / nyah
Sports and toys	Deportes y juguetes	deh-por-tehs-ee-hoh-geh-tehs
Thanks a million	Mil gracias	meel-grah-thee-ass
There is	Hay	eye
They are very pretty	Son muy bonitos / tas	son-mwee-boh-nee-tos / tas
To sell	Vender	ben-der
Where can I buy?	¿Dónde puedo comprar	don-deh-pweh-doh-kom-prar
Which one do you prefer?	¿Cuál prefieres?	kwal-preh-fee-eh-rehs
Which one do you want?	¿Cuál quieres?	kwal-kee-eh-rehs

Learn Spanish In One Week

Medicine

English	Spanish	Pronunciation
Antibiotic	El antibiótico	an-tee-bee-oh-tee-koh
Aspirin	La aspirina	ass-pee-ree-nah
Cough medicine	El medicamento para la tos	meh-dee-kah-men-toh-pah-rah-lah-toss
Cough medicine	La medicina para la tos	meh-dee-thee-nah-pah-rah-lah-toss
Cough syrup	El jarabe para la tos	hah-rah-beh-pah-rah-lah-toss
Ear infection	La infección de oído	een-fek-thee-on-deh-oh-ee-doh
Eye drops	El colirio	koh-lee-ree-oh
Eye drops	Las gotas para los ojos	goh-tas-pah-rah-los-oh-hohs
Fungal infection	La infección fúngica	een-fek-thee-on-foon-hee-kah
Indigestion	La indigestión	een-dee-hess-tee-on
Insect bite	Picadura de insecto	pee-kah-doo-rah-deh-een-sek-toh
Insect repellent	El repelente de insectos	reh-peh-len-teh-deh-een-sek-tos
Paracetamol	Paracetamol	pah-rah-theh-tah-mol
Plaster (Band-Aid)	La curita	koo-ree-tah
Plaster (Band-Aid) (Spain)	La tirita	tee-ree-tah
Penicillin		
Pulled muscle	El músculo desgarrado	moo-skoo-loh-des-hah-rah-doh
Sore throat	El dolor de garganta	doh-lor-deh-gar-gan-tah
Worms	Las lombrices	lom-bree-thehs

Learn Spanish In One Week

Months

English	Spanish	Pronunciation
January	enero	eh-neh-roh
February	febrero	feh-breh-roh
March	marzo	mar-thoh
April	abril	ah-breel
May	mayo	mah-yoh
June	junio	hoo-nee-oh
July	julio	hoo-lee-oh
August	agosto	ow-goos-toh
September	septiembre	sep-tee-em-breh
October	octubre	ohk-too-breh
November	noviembre	noh-bee-em-breh
December	diciembre	dee-thee-em-breh
In February	En febrero	en-feh-breh-roh
Last March	En marzo pasado	en-mar-thoh-pah-sah-doh
Last month	El mes pasado	el-mes-pah-sah-doh
My birthday is at the end of May	Mi cumpleaños es a finales de mayo	mee-koom-pleh-ah-nyoss-es-ah-fee-nah-lehs-deh-mah-yoh
My father's birthday is the 9th of March	El cumpleaños de mi padre es el nueve de marzo	el-koom-pleh-ah-nyoss-de-mee-pah-dreh-es-el mweh-beh-deh-mar-thoh
Next month	El próximo mes	el-prok-see-moh-mess

Learn Spanish In One Week

Music

English	Spanish	Pronunciation
Accordion	El acordeón	ah-kor-deh-on
Bagpipes	La gaita	geye-tah
Banjo	El banjo / El banyo	ban-hoh / ban-yoh
Basson	El fagot	fah-got
Cello	El cello	theh-yoh
Clarinet	El clarinete	klah-ree-neh-teh
Concert	El concierto	kon-thee-er-toh
Double bass	El contrabajo	kon-trah-bah-hoh
Drum	El tambor	tam-bor
Drums	La batería	bah-teh-ree-ah
French horn	El corno francés	kor-noh-fran-thehs
Flute	La flauta	fl-ow-tah
Guitar	La guitarra	gee-tah-rrah
Harp	El arpa	ar-pah
Keyboard	El teclado	teh-klah-doh
Microphone	El micrófono	mee-kroh-foh-noh
Music	La música	moo-see-kah
Musical instrument	El instrumento musical	eens-troo-men-toh-moo-see-kal
Musician	El músico	moo-see-koh
Oboe	El oboe	oh-boh-eh

Learn Spanish In One Week

English	Spanish	Pronunciation
Orchestra	La orquesta	or-kess-tah
Piano	El piano	pee-ah-noh
Piccolo	El flautín	fl-ow-teen ("ow" as in "how")
Platform	El estrado	es-trah-doh
Pop music	La música pop	moo-see-kah-pop
Recorder	La flauta dulce	fl-ow-tah-dool-theh
Saxophone	El saxofón	sak-soh-fohn
Sheet music	Las partituras	par-tee-too-ras
Sing a song	Cantar una canción	kan-tar-oo-nah-kan-thee-on
Song	La canción	kan-thee-on
Song	El canto	kan-toh
Stage	El escenario	es-theh-nah-ree-oh
Stage	El tablado	tah-blah-doh
Synthesiser	El sintetizador	seen-teh-tee-thah-dor
Trombone	El trombón	trom-bon
Trumpet	La trompeta	trom-peh-tah
Tuba	La tuba	too-bah
Ukelele	El ukelele	oo-keh-leh-leh
Violin	El violín	bee-oh-leen
Xylophone	El xilófono	ksee-loh-foh-noh

Learn Spanish In One Week

Nature

English	Spanish	Pronunciation
Antarctic	El antártico	an-tar-tee-koh
Beach	La playa	plah-yah
Cave	La cueva	kweh-bah
Cliff	El acantilado	ah-kan-tee-lah-doh
Coast	La costa	kos-tah
Coral reef	El arrecife de coral	ah-rreh-thee-feh-deh-koh-ral
Countryside	La campiña	kam-pee-nyah
Countryside	El campo	kam-poh
Desert	El desierto	deh-see-er-toh
Earthquake	El terremoto	teh-rreh-moh-toh
Environment	El medioambiente	meh-dee-oh-am-bee-en-teh
Field	La cancha	kan-chah
Forest	El bosque	bos-keh
Glacier	El glaciar	glah-thee-ar
Headland	La punta	poon-tah
Hill	La colina	koh-lee-nah
Iceberg	Iceberg	ee-theh-berg
Island	La isla	ees-lah
Jungle	La jungla	hoon-glah
Jungle	La selva	sel-bah

Learn Spanish In One Week

English	Spanish	Pronunciation
Lake	El lago	lah-goh
Land	La tierra	tee-eh-rah
Marsh	La ciénaga	thee-eh-nah-gah
Meadow	El prado	prah-doh
Moon	La luna	loo-nah
Moors	El páramo	pah-rah-moh
Mountain	La montaña	mon-tah-nyah
Ocean	El océano	oh-theh-ah-noh
Rainforest	La selva lluviosa	sel-bah-yoo-bee-oh-sah
Rainforest	La selva tropical	sel-bah-troh-pee-kal
River	El río	rree-oh
Sea	El / La mar	mar
Sky	El cielo	thee-eh-loh
Star	La estrella	es-trah-yah
Stream	El arroyo	ah-rroh-yoh
Stream / Brook	El riachuelo	ree-ah-chweh-loh
Sun	El sol	sol
Valley	El valle	bah-yeh
Volcano	El volcán	bol-kan
Woods	El bosque	boss-keh

Learn Spanish In One Week

Numbers

English	Spanish	Pronunciation
One	Uno	oo-noh
Two	Dos	dos
Three	Tres	trehs
Four	Cuatro	kwah-troh
Five	Cinco	theen-koh
Six	Seis	sehs
Seven	Siete	see-eh-teh
Eight	Ocho	oh-choh
Nine	Nueve	nweh-beh
Ten	Diez	dee-eth
Eleven	Once	on-theh
Twelve	Doce	doh-theh
Thirteen	Trece	treh-theh
Fourteen	Catorce	kah-tor-theh
Fifteen	Quince	keen-theh
Sixteen	Dieciséis	dee-eh-thee-sehs
Seventeen	Diecisiete	dee-eh-thee-see-eh-teh
Eighteen	Dieciocho	dee-eh-thee-oh-choh
Nineteen	Diecinueve	dee-eh-thee-nweh-beh
Twenty	Veinte	beh-n-teh

Learn Spanish In One Week

English	Spanish	Pronunciation
Twenty one	Ventiuno	beh-n-tee-oo-noh
Twenty two	Ventidós	beh-n-tee-dos
Thirty	Treinta	treh-n-tah
Thirty one	Treinta y uno	treh-n-tah-ee-oo-noh
Thirty two	Treinta y dos	treh-n-tah-ee-dos
Forty	Cuarenta	kwah-ren-tah
Forty one	Cuarenta y uno	kwah-ren-tah-ee-oo-noh
Forty five	Cuarenta y cinco	kwah-ren-tah-ee-theen-koh
Fifty	Cinquenta	theen-kwen-tah
Sixty	Sesenta	seh-sen-tah
Seventy	Setenta	seh-ten-tah
Eighty	Ochenta	oh-chen-tah
Ninety	Noventa	noh-ben-tah
One hundred	Cien	thee-en
One hundred and one	Ciento uno	thee-en-toh-oo-noh
One hundred and two	Ciento dos	thee-en-toh-dos
One thousand	Mil	meel
Ten thousand	Diez mil	dee-eth-meel
One million	Un millión	oon-mee-yon
One billion	Mil millones	meel-mee-yoh-nehs

Learn Spanish In One Week

Office

English	Spanish	Pronunciation
Agenda (meeting)	La agenda	ah-hen-dah
Bin	La papelera	pah-peh-leh-rah
Boss	El jefe / La jefa	heh-feh / heh-fah
Business card	La tarjeta de negocios	tar-heh-tah-deh-neh-goh-thee-ohs
Business card	La tarjeta de visita	tar-heh-tah-deh-bee-see-tah
Businessman	El hombres de negocios	om-breh-deh-neh-goh-thee-ohs
Business owner	El empresario	em-preh-sah-ree-oh
Businesswoman	La mujer de negocios	moo-her-deh-neh-goh-thee-ohs
Colleague	El / La colega	koh-leh-dah
Colleague	El compañero	kon-pah-nyeh-roh
Computer	La computadora	kom-poo-tah-doh-rah
Cost	El costo	kohs-toh
Deadline	La fecha de entrega	feh-chah-deh-en-treh-gah
Decision	La decisión	deh-thee-see-on
Desk	El escritorio	es-kree-toh-ree-oh
Director	Director	dee-rek-tor
Document	El documento	doh-koo-men-toh
Envelope	El sobre	soh-breh
Fax	El fax	fahks
Fax number	El número de fax	noo-meh-roh-deh-fahks

Learn Spanish In One Week

English	Spanish	Pronunciation
File	El archivo	ar-chee-boh
Folder	La carpeta	kar-peh-tah
I'm busy	Estoy ocupado/a	es-toy-oh-koo-pah-doh / dah
Incentive	El incentivo	een-th-en-tee-boh
Ink	La tinta	teen-tah
Internet	El / La internet	een-ter-net
Internet connection	La conexión de internet	koh-nek-see-on-deh-een-ter-net
Interview	La entrevista	en-treh-bees-tah
Label	La etiqueta	eh-tee-keh-tah
Laptop	La laptop	lap-top
Machine	La máquina	mah-kee-nah
Management	La dirección	dee-rek-thee-on
Management	La gerencia	heh-ren-thee-ah
Meeting / Appointment	La cita	thee-tah
Meeting	La reunión	reh-oo-nee-on
Meeting room	La sala de reuniones	sah-lah-deh-reh-oo-nee-on-ehs
Money	El dinero	dee-neh-roh
Office	La oficina	oh-fee-thee-nah
Paper	El papel	pah-pel
Pen	El bolígrafo	boh-lee-grah-foh

Learn Spanish In One Week

English	Spanish	Pronunciation
Pen	La pluma	ploo-mah
Pencil	El lápiz	lah-peeth
Phone	El teléfono	teh-leh-foh-noh
Phone call	La llamada	yah-mah-dah
Photocopier	La fotocopiadora	foh-toh-koh-pee-ah-doh-rah
Presentation	La presentación	preh-sen-tah-thee-on
Price	El precio	preh-thee-oh
Printer	La impresora	eem-preh-soh-rah
Scanner	El escáner	es-kah-ner
Sellotape	La cinta adhesiva	theen-tah-ad-eh-see-bah
Sellotape	El celo	theh-loh
Stapler	La grapadora	grah-pah-doh-rah
Staples	La grapa	grah-pah
Strategy	La estrategia	es-trah-teh-hee-ah
To file	Archivar	ar-chee-bar
Updates	Las últimas noticias	ool-tee-mas-noh-tee-thee-ass
Videoconference	Videoconferencia	bee-dee-oh-kon-feh-ren-thee-ah
We'll see each other soon	Nos vemos pronto	nos-beh-moss-pron-toh

Learn Spanish In One Week

Ordinals

English	Spanish	Pronunciation
First	Primero / a	pree-meh-roh / pree-meh-rah
Second	Segundo	seh-goon-doh / seh-goon-dah
Third	Tercero / a	ter-theh-roh / ter-theh-rah
Fourth	Cuarto / a	kwar-toh / kwar-tah
Fifth	Quinto / a	keen-toh- / keen-tah
Sixth	Sexto / a	seks-toh / seks-tah
Seventh	Séptimo / a	sep-tee-moh / sep-tee-mah
Eighth	Octavo / a	ohk-tak-boh / ohk-tah-bah
Ninth	Noveno / a	noh-beh-noh / noh-beh-nah
Tenth	Décimo / a	deh-thee-moh / deh-thee-mah
First floor	Primer piso	pree-mer-pee-soh
Second hand	Segundero	seh-goon-deh-roh
Third word	El tercer mundo	ter-ther-moon-doh
Fourth day	Cuarto día	kwar-toh-dee-ah
Fifth avenue	La quinta avenida	keen-tah-ah-beh-nee-dah
Sixth grade	Sexto grado	seks-toh-grah-doh
Seventh floor	Séptimo piso	sep-tee-moh-pee-soh
Eighth largest	Octavo más grande	ock-tah-boh-mas-gran-deh
Ninth grade	Noveno grado	noh-beh-noh-grah-doh
Tenth floor	Décimo piso	deh-thee-moh-pee-soh

Learn Spanish In One Week

Personal Details

English	Spanish	Pronunciation
Address	La dirección	dee-rek-thee-on
Age	La edad	eh-dad
Date	La fecha	feh-chah
First name	El nombre de pila	nom-breh-deh-pee-lah
Flight number	El número de vuelo	noo-meh-roh-deh-bweh-loh
Home address	La dirección particular	dee-rek-thee-on-par-tee-koo-lar
Last name	El apellido	ah-peh-yee-doh
Madam / Ma'am / Woman	La señora	seh-nyor-ah
Miss	La señorita	seh-nyor-ree-tah
Mr	El señor / El Sr.	seh-nyor / seh-nyor
Mrs	La señora / La Sra.	seh-nyor-ah / seh-nyor-ah
Name	El nombre	nom-breh
Nationality	La nacionalidad	nah-thee-oh-nah-lee-dad
Occupation	La ocupación	oh-koo-pah-thee-on
Occupation	La profesión	proh-feh-see-on
Signature	La firma	feer-mah
Sir / man / gentleman	El señor	seh-nyor
To vaccinate	Vacunar	bah-koo-nar
Vaccinated	Vacunarme	bah-koo-nar-meh
Young lady / woman	La señorita	seh-nyor-ree-tah

Learn Spanish In One Week

Police

English	Spanish	Pronunciation
Armed robbery	El robo a mano armada	el-roh-boh-ah-mah-noh-ar-mah-dah
Attacker	El / La agresor/a	ah-greh-sor / ah-greh-soh-rah
Badge	La placa	plah-kah
Baton	La porra	ph-rrah
Burglary	El robo	roh-boh
Clue	La pista	pees-tah
Crime (serious)	El crimen	kree-men
Crime (less serious)	El delito	deh-lee-toh
Criminal	El / La criminal	kree-mee-nal
Criminal / delinquent	El / La delincuente	deh-leen-kwen-teh
Dead	Muerto	mwer-toh
Death	Muerte	mwer-teh
Gun	La pistola	pees-toh-lah
Handcuffs	Las esposas	es-poh-sas
Harassment	El acoso	ah-koh-soh
Homicide	El homicidio	oh-mee-thee-dee-oh
Interrogation	El interrogatorio	een-teh-rroh-gah-toh-ree-oh
Investigation	La investigación	een-bes-tee-gah-thee-on
Intruder	El / La intruso/a	een-troo-soh / sah

Learn Spanish In One Week

English	Spanish	Pronunciation
Murder	El asesinato	ah-seh-see-nah-toh
Murderer	El / La asesino/a	ah-seh-see-noh / nah
Police	La policía	poh-lee-thee-ah
Police car	El coche de policía	koh-cheh-de-poh-lee-thee-ah
Police officer	El / la policía	poh-lee-thee-ah
Police officer	El / La agente de policía	ah-hen-teh-deh-poh-lee-thee-ah
Police station	La comisaría	koh-mee-sah-ree-ah
Police station	La estación de policía	es-tah-thee-on-deh-poh-lee-thee-ah
Police superintendent	El / La comisario/a	koh-mee-sah-ree-oh / rah
Private investigator	El / La detective privado/a	deh-tek-tee-beh-pree-bah-doh / dah
Rape	La violación	bee-oh-lah-thee-on
Rapist	El / La violador/a	bee-oh-lah-dor / doh-rah
Show me your hands	Muéstrame las manos	mwess-trah-meh-las-mah-nos
Sexual assault	La agresión sexual	ah-greh-see-on-sek-swal
Sexual harassment	El acoso sexual	ah-koh-soh-sek-swal
Stalker	El / La acosador/a	ah-koh-sah-dor / doh-rah
Stalking	El acoso	ah-koh-soh
Suspect	El / La sospechoso/a	sos-peh-choh-soh / sah
Theft / Robbery	El robo	roh-boh

Learn Spanish In One Week

English	Spanish	Pronunciation
Thief / Robber	El ladrón / La ladrona	lah-dron / lah-droh-nah
To arrest / To detain	Detener	deh-teh-ner
To chase	Perseguir	per-seh-geer
To handcuff	Esposar	es-poh-sar
To harass	Acosar	ah-koh-sar
To interrogate	Interrogar	een-teh-rroh-gar
To investigate	Investigar	een-bes-tee-gar
To kill	Asesinar	ah-seh-see-nar
To kill	Matar	mah-tar
To murder	Asesinar	ah-seh-see-nar
To patrol	Patrullar	pah-troo-yar
To rape	Violar	bee-oh-lar
To shoot	Disparar	dees-pah-rar
To steal / To rob	Robar	rroh-bar
Victim	La víctima	beek-tee-mah
What is your name?	¿cuál es su nombre?	kwal-es-soo-nom-breh
Where you you live (formal)	¿Dónde vive?	don-deh-bee-beh
Witness	El / La testigo	tes-tee-goh
You can't	No puede	noh-pweh-deh

Learn Spanish In One Week

Pronouns

English	Spanish	Pronunciation
Demonstrative Pronouns		
This / This one	Este / Esta	es-teh . es-tah
These / These ones	Estos / Estas	es-tos / es-tas
That / That one	Ese / Esa	eh-seh-eh-sah
That one over there	Aquel / Aquella	ah-kel / ah-keh-yah
Those / Those ones	Esos / Esas	eh-sos / eh-sas
Those ones over there	Aquellos / Aquellas	ah-keh-yos / ah-keh-yas
I want this one	Quiero este	kee-eh-roh-es-teh
She bought this one	Ella compró este	eh-yah-kom-proh-es-teh
I want that one	Quiero ese	kee-eh-roh-eh-seh
She likes that one	A ella le gusta ese	ah-eh-yah-leh-goos-tah-es-seh
Which car do you want?	¿Qué coche quieres?	keh-koh-cheh-kee-eh-rehs
That one over there	Aquel	ah-kel
Direct Object Pronouns		
Me	Me / Mí	meh/ mee
You	Te	teh
Him / Her / It	Lo / La	loh / lah
Us	Nos	noss

Learn Spanish In One Week

English	Spanish	Pronunciation
You	Os	oss
Them	Los / Las	loss / lass
For me	Para mí	pah-rah-mee
I can finish it	La. puedo. terminar	lah-pweh-doh-ter-mee-nar
I can't see him	No lo puedo ver	noh-loh-pweh-doh-ber
I can't see you	No te puedo ver	noh-teh-pweh-doh-ber
I love you	Te amo	teh-ah-moh
I see him	Lo veo	loh-beh-oh
Indefinite Pronouns		
Singular		
Anybody	Alguien	al-gee-en
Anyone	Cualquiera	kwal-kee-eh-rah
Anything / Nothing	Nada	nah-dah
Each / Everyone	Cada uno / Cada una	kah-dah-oo-noh / kah-dah-oo-nah
Either	Cualquiera	kwal-kee-eh-rah
Neither	Ninguno	neen-goo-noh
Nobody / No one	Nadie	nah-dee-eh
Somebody / Someone	Alguien	al-gee-en
Something	Algo	al-goh

Learn Spanish In One Week

English	Spanish	Pronunciation
Plural		
Both	Ambos	am-bos
Few	Pocos	poh-kohs
Many	Muchos	moo-chohs
Several	Varios	bah-ree-ohs
Single or Plural		
All	Todo	toh-doh
Any	Alguno/a	al-goo-noh / nah
Most	La mayoría de	lah-mah-yoh-ree-ah-deh
Some / A little	Un poco	oon-poh-koh
Some	Algunos / Algunas	al-goo-nohs / al-goo-nas
Indirect Object Pronouns		
Me	Me	meh
You	Te	teh
Him / Her	Le / Se	leh / seh
Us	Nos	noss
You	Les	less
Them	Les	less
Interrotagive Pronouns		
What	Qué	keh

Learn Spanish In One Week

English	Spanish	Pronunciation
Who	Quién	kee-en
Which	Cuál	kwal
Whom	Quién	kee-en
Whose	De quién	deh-kee-en
Personal Pronouns		
I	Yo	joh
You (singular)	Tú	too
He / She / It	Él / Ella	el / eh-yah
We	Nosotros / Nosotras	noh-soh-tros / noh-soh-tras
You (plural)	Ustedes	oos-ted-ehs
They	Ellos / Ellas	eh-yoss / eh-yass
I am not French	Yo no soy francés	joh-noh-soy-fran-thehs
You are very intelligent	Tú eres muy inteligente	too-eh-rehs-mwee-een-teh-lee-hen-teh
It is new	Él es nuevo	el-es-nweh-boh
We are going to win	Nosotros vamos a ganar	noh-soh-tros-bah-mos-ah-gah-nar
They are married	Ellos están casados	eh-yoss-es-tan-kah-sah-dos
Possessive Pronouns		
Mine	Mío /Mía / Míos / Mías	mee-oh / mee-ah / mee-os / mee-ass
Yours	Tuyo / Tuya / Tuyos / Tuyas	too-you / too-yah / too-yos / too-yas

Learn Spanish In One Week

English	Spanish	Pronunciation
His / Hers / Its	Suyo / Suya / Suyos / Suyas	soo-yoh / soo-yah / soo-yos / soo-yas
Ours	Nuestro / Nuestra / Nuestros / Nuestras	nwes-troh / nwes-trah / nwes-trohs-nwes-tras
Yours	Vuestro / Vuestra / Vuestros / Vuestras	bwes-troh / bwes-trah / bwes-trohs / bwes-tras
Theirs	Suyo / Suya / Suyos / Suyas	soo-yoh / soo-yah / soo-yos / soo-yas
It's mine	Es mío / Es el mío	es-mee-oh / es-el-mee-oh
It's ours	Es nuestro / Es el nuestro	es-nwes-troh / es-el-nwes-troh
My	Mi / Mis	mee / mees
Your	Tu / Tus	too / toos
His / Her / It	Su / Sus	soo / soos
Our	Nuestro / Nuestra / Nuestros / Nuestras	nwes-troh / nwes-trah / nwes-trohs / nwes-tras
Your	Vuestro / Vuestra / Vuestros / Vuestras	bwes-troh / bwes-trah / bwes-trohs / bwes-tras
Their	Sun / Sus	soo / soos
My house	Mi casa	mee-kah-sah
This is my wife	Ésta es mi esposa	es-tah-es-mee-es-poh-sah
Your car	Tu coche	too-koh-cheh
His girlfriend	Su novia	soo-noh-bee-ah
This is his	Este es su	es-teh-es-soo
Our garden	Nuestro jardín	nwes-troh-har-deen

Learn Spanish In One Week

English	Spanish	Pronunciation
Their holiday	Sus vacaciones	soos-bah-kah-thee-on-ehs
Reflexive Pronouns		
Myself	Me	meh
Yourself	Te	teh
Himself / Herself / Itself	Se	seh
Ourselves	Nos	nos
Yourselves	Os	os
Themselves	Se	seh
I bathe myself	Me baño	meh-bah-nyoh
I wake myself	Me despierto	meh-des-pee-er-toh
Relative Pronouns		
That / Which / Who	Que	keh
Who	Quien	kee-en
That / Which / Who	El cual	el-kwal
What / Which	Lo que	loh-keh
Whose	Cuyo	koo-yoh
I don't know what I want	No sé lo que quiero	noh-seh-loh-keh-kee-eh-roh
Who made dinner	Quién preparó la cena	kee-en-preh-pah-roh-lah-theh-nah
What I don't understand	Lo que no entiendo es	loh-keh-no-en-tee-en-doh-es

Learn Spanish In One Week

Questions

English	Spanish	Pronunciation
Are you married?	¿Estás casado?	es-tas-kah-sah-doh
Are you sure?	¿Estás seguro?	es-tas-seh-goo-roh
Can I ask you a question?	¿Puedo hacerte una pregunta?	pweh-doh-ah-ther-teh-oo-nah-preh-goon-tah
Do you agree?	¿Estás de acuerdo?	es-tas-deh-ah-kwer-doh
Do you have?	¿Tienes?	tee-en-ehs
Do you have a boyfriend?	¿Tienes novio?	tee-en-ehs-noh-bee-oh
Do you speak Spanish?	¿Hablas español?	ah-blass-es-pah-nyol
From where?	¿De dónde?	deh-don-deh
How?	¿Cómo?	koh-moh
How did you do that?	¿Cómo hiciste eso?	koh-moh-ee-thee-steh-eh-soh
How is?	¿Cómo es / Cómo está?	koh-moh-es / koh-moh-es-tah
How is everyone?	¿Cómo están todos?	koh-moh-es-tan-toh-dos
How is everything?	¿Cómo está todo?	koh-moh-es-tah-toh-doh
How many?	¿Cuántos / Cuántas?	kwan-toss / kwan-tass
How many do you want?	¿Cuántos quieres?	kwan-toss-kee-eh-rehs
How much?	¿Cuánto / Cuánta?	kwan-toh / kwan-tah
How much tea?	¿Cuánto té?	kwan-toh-teh
How much water?	¿Cuánto agua?	kwan-toh-ah-gwah
Question	La pregunta	preh-goon-teh

Learn Spanish In One Week

English	Spanish	Pronunciation
What?	¿Qué / Cuál?	keh / kwal
What are you doing?	¿Qué haces?	keh-ah-thehs
What are you doing right now?	¿Qué haces ahora mismo?	keh-ah-thehs-ah-oh-rah-mees-moh
What day is it?	¿Qué día es?	keh-dee-ah-es
What does he want?	¿Qué quiere?	keh-kee-eh-reh
What do you think?	¿Qué piensas?	keh-pee-en-sas
What for?	Para qué	pah-rah-keh
What's that?	¿Qué es eso?	keh-es-eh-soh
What's that noise?	¿Cuál es ese ruido?	kwal-es-es-eh-roo-ee-doh
What is this for?	¿Para qué es eso?	pah-rah-keh-es-es-oh
What is your favourite movie?	¿Cuál es ti película favorita?	kwal-es-too-peh-lee-koo-lah-fah-boh-ree-tah
When?	¿Cuándo?	kwan-doh
When are you coming back?	¿Cuándo vuelves?	kwan-doh-bwel-behs
When is the party?	¿Cuándo es la fiesta?	kwan-doh-es-lah-fee-es-tah
When is your birthday?	¿Cuándo es tu cumpleaños?	kwan-doh-es-too-koom-pleh-ah-nyoss
When will you return?	¿Cuándo volverás?	kwan-doh-bol-beh-ras
Where?	¿Dónde?	don-deh
Where are the keys?	¿Dónde están las llaves?	don-deh-es-tan-las-yah-behs

Learn Spanish In One Week

English	Spanish	Pronunciation
Where are you?	¿Dónde estás?	don-deh-es-tas
Where are you going?	¿A dónde vas?	ah-don-deh-bas
Where is the bank?	¿Dónde está el banco?	don-deh-es-tah-el-ban-koh
Where to?	¿Adónde?	ah-don-deh
Which?	¿Cuál?	kwal
Which is your favourite?	¿Cuál es tu favorito?	kwal-es-too-fah-boh-ree-toh
Which one do you prefer?	¿Cuál prefieres?	kwal-preh-fee-eh-rehs
Which one do you want?	¿Cuál quieres?	kwal-kee-eh-rehs
Who	¿Quién / Quiénes?	kee-en / kee-eh-nehs
Who are you?	¿Quién eres?	kee-en-eh-rehs
Who are they?	¿Quiénes son?	kee-eh-nehs-son
Who are you thinking about?	¿En quién estás pensando?	en-kee-en-es-tas-pen-san-doh
Who is it?	¿Quién es?	kee-en-es
Whose?	¿De quién?	deh-kee-en
Whose is that house?	¿De quién es esa casa?	deh-kee-en-es-eh-sah-kah-sah
Why?	¿Por qué?	por-keh
Why are they here?	¿Por qué están aquí?	por-keh-es-tan-ah-kee
Why are you nervous?	¿Por qué estás nervioso?	por-keh-es-tas-ner-bee-oh-soh
Why do you say that?	¿Por qué dices eso?	por-keh-dee-thehs-eh-soh

Learn Spanish In One Week

Restaurant

English	Spanish	Pronunciation
Á la carte	A la carta	ah-lah-kar-tah
Appetite	El apetito	ah-peh-tee-toh
A table for four please	Una mesa para cuatro por favor	oo-nah-meh-sah-pah-rah-kwah-troh-por-fah-bor
Breakfast	ÉL desayuno	deh-sah-yoo-noh
By the window	Al lado de la ventana	al-lah-doh-deh-lah-ben-tah-nah
By the window	Junto a la ventana	hoon-toh-ah-lah-ben-tah-nah
Can I see the menu?	¿Puedo ver la carta?	pweh-doh-ber-lah-kar-tah
Can I see the menu?	¿Puedo ver el menú?	pweh-doh-ver-el-meh-noo
Cashier	El cajero / La cajera	kah-heh-roh / kah-heh-rah
Cheers	Salud	sah-lood
Chinese food	La comida china	koh-mee-dah-chee-nah
Closed on Mondays	Cerrado los lunes	ther-rah-doh-los-loo-nehs
Daily special	Especial del día	es-peh-thee-al-del-dee-ah
Desert	Postre	pos-treh
Dish of the day	Plato del día	plah-toh-del-dee-ah
Drink	La bebida	beh-bee-dah
Enjoy your meal	Buen provecho	bwen-proh-beh-choh
Excuse me	Perdone	per-doh-neh
Fast food	La comida rápida	koh-mee-dah-rah-pee-dah

Learn Spanish In One Week

English	Spanish	Pronunciation
Fixed price	El precio fijo	preh-thee-oh-fee-hoh
For two people	Para dos personas	pah-rah-dos-per-soh-nas
Happy hour	La hora feliz	lah-oh-rah-feh-leeth
Here's your change	Aquí está su cambio	ah-kee-es-tah-soo-kam-bee-oh
I don't eat meat	No como carne	noh-koh-moh-kar-neh
I have a reservation	Tengo una reserva	ten-goh-oo-nah-reh-ser-bah
In the restaurant	En el restaurante	en-el-res-tow-ran-teh
It's disgusting	Está asqueroso	es-tah-ass-keh-roh-soh
Main course	El plato fuerte	plah-toh-fwer-teh
Manager	El / La gerente	heh-ren-teh
Medium (steak)	Medio hecho	meh-dee-oh-eh-choh
Medium (steak)	Término medio	ter-mee-noh-meh-dee-oh
Napkin	La servilleta	ser-bee-yeh-tah
Nothing more	Nada más	nah-dah-mas
Rare (steak)	Poco hecho	poh-koh-eh-choh
Separate bills	Cuentas separadas	kwen-tas-seh-pah-rah-das
Spanish food	La comida española	koh-mee-dah-es-pah-nyol-lah
Starter	La entrada	en-trah-dah
Starter	El primer plato	pree-mer-plah-toh
Tasty	Sabroso	sah-broh-soh

Learn Spanish In One Week

English	Spanish	Pronunciation
The bill	La cuenta	kwen-tah
The desert menu	El menú de postres	el-meh-noo-deh-pos-trehs
The soup is cold	La sopa está fría	lah-soh-pah-es-tah-free-ah
Tip	La propina	proh-pee-nah
Turkish food	La comida turca	koh-mee-dah-toor-kah
Vegetarian menu	Menú vegetariano	meh-noo-beh-heh-tah-ree-ah-noh
Waiter	Camarero / Camarera	kah-mah-reh-roh / rah
Well done (steak)	Bien cocido	bee-en-koh-thee-doh
Well done (steak)	Bien hecho	bee-en-eh-choh
Well done (steak)	Muy hecho	mwee-eh-choh
What do you recommend?	¿Qué me recomiendas?	keh-meh-reh-koh-mee-en-das
What do you want?	¿Qué quieres?	keh-kee-eh-rehs
What would you like to drink?	¿Qué desea beber?	keh-deh-seh-ah-beh-ber
What would you like to eat?	¿Qué desea comer?	keh-deh-seh-ah-koh-mer
Wine cellar	La bodega	boh-deh-gah
Wine glass	La copa de vino	koh-pah-deh-bee-noh
Wine list	La carta de vinos	lah-kar-tah-deh-bee-nos
Yes sir	Si señor	see-seh-nyor

Learn Spanish In One Week

School

English	Spanish	Pronunciation
Absent	Ausente	ow-sen-teh
A-levels	Bachillerato	bah-chee-yeh-rah-toh
Answer	Respuesta	rehs-pwes-tah
Art	El arte	ar-teh
Assessment	La evaluacción	eh-bah-lwah-thee-on
Biology	La biología	bee-oh-loh-hee-ah
Blackboard	La pizarra	pee-thah-rah
Book	El libro	lee-broh
Boarding school	El internado	een-ter-nah-doh
Boarding school	El pensionado	pen-see-oh-nah-doh
Break	Descanso	des-kan-soh
Business studies	La administración de empresas	ad-mee-nee-strah-thee-on-deh-em-preh-sas
Calculator	La calculadora	kal-koo-lah-doh-rah
Canteen	La cantina	kan-tee-nah
Careers adviser	El orientador/a	oh-ree-en-tah-dor / doh-rah
Caretaker	El / La conserje	kon-ser-heh
Changing room	El vestuario	bes-twah-ree-oh
Chemistry	La química	kee-mee-kah
Choir	El coro	koh-roh

Learn Spanish In One Week

English	Spanish	Pronunciation
Class register	Registro de clase	reh-hee-stroh-deh-klah-seh
Class test	Prueba	proo-eh-bah
Classroom	La aula	ow-lah
Corridor	El corredor	koh-rreh-dor
Corridor	El pasillo	pah-see-yoh
Degree (University)	El título	tee-too-loh
Desk	La mesa de trabajo	meh-sah-deh-trah-bah-hoh
Desk	El pupitre	poo-pee-treh
Detention	El castigo	kass-tee-goh
Dictionary	El diccionario	deek-thee-oh-nah-ree-oh
Drama	El arte dramático	ar-teh-drah-mah-tee-koh
Drawing	El dibujo	dee-boo-hoh
Design Technology	Diseño y tecnología	dee-seh-nyoh-ee-tek-nol-oh-hee-oh
Earphones	Los auriculares	ow-ree-koo-lah-rehs
Economics	La economía	eh-koh-noh-mee-ah
Education	La educación	eh-doo-kah-thee-on
English	Inglés	een-glehs
Essay	El ensayo	en-sah-yoh
Essay	La redacción	rreh-dak-thee-on

Learn Spanish In One Week

English	Spanish	Pronunciation
Examination	El examen	ek-sah-men
Exam paper	La hoja de examen	oh-hah-deh-ek-sah-men
Exercise book	Él cuaderno	kwah-der-noh
Experiment	El experimento	eks-peh-ree-men-toh
Felt tip	El rotulador	rroh-too-lah-dor
Final exam	El examen final	ek-sah-men-fee-nal
Food technology	Technología de los alimentos	tek-noh-loh-hee-ah-deh-los-ah-lee-men-tos
Foreign language	El idioma extranjero	ee-dee-oh-mah-eks-tran-heh-roh
Foreign language	La lengua extranjera	len-gwah-eks-tran-heh-rah
Fountain pen	La pluma estilográfica	ploo-mah-es-tee-loh-grah-fee-kah
French	Francés	fran-thehs
Geography	Geografía	hee-oh-grah-fee-ah
German	Alemán	ah-leh-man
Glue	La goma	goh-mah
Glue	El pegamento	peh-gah-men-toh
Gym	El gimnasio	heem-nah-see-oh
Gymnastics	La gimnasia	heem-nah-see-ah
Half-term	Las vacaciones de mitad de trimestre	bah-kah-thee-on-ehs-deh-mee-tad-deh-tree-meh-streh

Learn Spanish In One Week

English	Spanish	Pronunciation
Headphones	El audíofono	ow-dee-foh-noh
Head teacher	El director	dee-rek-tor
History	La historia	ees-toh-ree-ah
Homework	Los deberes	deh-beh-rehs
Humanities	Las humanidades	oo-man-ee-dah-dehs
Ink cartridge	El cartucho de tinta	kat-too-choh-deh-teen-tah
Italian	Italiano	ee-tah-lee-ah-noh
Laboratory	El laboratorio	lah-boh-rah-toh-ree-oh
Language lab	Laboratorio de idiomas	lah-boh-rah-toh-ree-oh-deh-ee-dee-oh-mas
Latin	El latín	lah-teen
Library	La biblioteca	bee-blee-oh-teh-kah
Lunch break	El descanso para almorzar	des-kan-soh-pah-rah-al-mor-thar
Mark / Grade	La nota	noh-tah
Maths	Las matemáticas	mah-teh-mah-tee-kas
Music	La música	moo-see-kah
Pad of paper	La bloc de notas	blok-deh-noh-tas
Page	La página	pah-hee-nah
Parents evening	Noche de padres	noh-cheh-deh-pah-drehs
Pen	El bolígrafo	boh-lee-grah-foh

Learn Spanish In One Week

English	Spanish	Pronunciation
Pen	La pluma	ploo-mah
Pencil	El lápiz	lah-peeth
Pencil case	El estuche	es-too-cheh
Physical education	La educación física	eh-doo-kah-thee-on-fee-see-kah
Physics	La física	fee-see-kah
Playground	El patio de recreo	pah-tee-oh-deh-reh-kreh-oh
Private school	El colegio privado	koh-leh-hee-oh-pree-bah-doh
Private school	La escuela privada	es-kweh-lah-pree-bah-dah
Pronunciation	La pronunciación	proh-noon-thee-ah-thee-on
Pupil	El alumno	ah-loom-noh
Qualification	La calificación	kah-lee-fee-kah-thee-on
Report	El reportaje	rreh-por-tah-heh
Result	El resultado	rreh-sool-tah-doh
Rubber	La goma	goh-mah
Rule	La regla	rreh-glah
Ruler	La regla	rreh-glah
School	El colegio	koh-leh-hee-oh
School	La escuela	es-kweh-lah
School	El instituto	eens-tee-too-toh

Learn Spanish In One Week

English	Spanish	Pronunciation
School bag	La cartera	kar-teh-rah
School bag	La mochila	moh-chee-lah
School book / Text book	El libro de texto	lee-broh-deh-teks-toh
School bus	El autobús escolar	ow-toh-boos-es-koh-lar
School certificate	El certificado	ther-tee-fee-kah-doh
School day	El día escolar	dee-ah-es-koh-lar
School friend	Amigo de la escuela	ah-mee-goh-deh-lah-es-kweh-lah
School friend	Camarada	kah-mah-rah-dah
School group	El grupo escolar	groo-poh-es-koh-lar
School office	El despacho	des-pah-choh
School office	Oficina de la escuela	oh-fee-thee-nah-deh-lah-es-kweh-lah
School report	El boletín de notas	boh-leh-teen-deh-noh-tas
School trip	La excursión del colegio	eks-koor-see-on-del-koh-leh-hee-oh
School uniform	El uniforme escolar	oo-nee-for-meh-es-koh-lar
School year	El año escolar	ah-nyoh-es-koh-lar
Science	La ciencia	thee-en-thee-ah
Scissors	Las tijeras	tee-heh-ras
Semester	El semestre	seh-mes-treh

Learn Spanish In One Week

English	Spanish	Pronunciation
Sharpener	El sacapuntas	sah-kah-poon-tas
Sociology	La sociología	soh-thee-oh-loh-hee-ah
Spanish	Español	es-pah-nyol
Sports field	El campo de deportes	kam-poh-deh-deh-por-tehs
Staff room	La sala de profesores	sah-lah-deh-proh-feh-soh-rehs
State School	La escuela pública	es-kweh-lah-poo-blee-kah
Student	El / La estudiante	es-too-dee-an-teh
Studies	Los estudios	es-too-dee-ohs
Subject	La asignatura	ah-seeg-nah-too-rah
Success	Éxito	ek-see-toh
Successful	Exitoso/a	ek-see-toh-soh / sah
Summer holidays	Vacaciones del verano	bah-kah-thee-oh-nehs-del-beh-rah-noh
Teacher	El profesor / El maestro	proh-feh-sor / mah-es-troh
Team	El equipo	eh-kee-poh
Technology	La tecnología	tek-noh-loh-hee-ah
Term	Él trimestre	tree-mes-treh
Test	La prueba	preh-bah
Text book	El libro de texto	lee-broh-deh-teks-toh
Timetable	El horario	oh-rah-ree-oh

Learn Spanish In One Week

Shapes

English	Spanish	Pronunciation
Arch	El arco	ar-koh
Circle	El círculo	theer-koo-loh
Cross	La cruz	krooth
Crescent	La medialuna	meh-dee-ah-loo-nah
Cube	El cubo	koo-boh
Diamond	El diamante	dee-ah-man-teh
Heart	El corazón	koh-rah-thon
Hexagon	El hexágono	ek-sah-goh-noh
Octagon	El octágono	ock-tah-goh-noh
Oval	El óvalo	oh-bah-loh
Pentagon	El pentágono	pen-tah-goh-noh
Pyramid	El pirámide	pee-rah-mee-deh
Rectangle	Rectángulo	rek-tan-goo-loh
Semicircle	El semicírculo	seh-mee-theer-koo-loh
Shape	La forma	for-mah
Spiral	El espiral	es-pee-ral
Square	El cuadrado	kwah-drah-doh
Star	La estrella	es-treh-yah
Triangle	El triángulo	tree-an-goo-loh
Trapezium	El trapecio	trah-peh-thee-oh

Learn Spanish In One Week

Ships and Boats

English	Spanish	Pronunciation
Anchor	El ancla	an-klah
Beam	La manga	man-gah
Boat	El barco	bar-koh
Boat (small)	El bote	boh-teh
Boom	La botavara	boh-tah-bah-rah
Bow	La proa	proh-ah
Bridge	El puente de mando	pwen-teh-deh-man-doh
Buoy	La boya	boh-yah
Cabin	La camarote	kah-mah-roh-teh
Captain	El capitán	kah-pee-tan
Catamaran	El catamarán	kah-tah-mah-ran
Compass	La brújula	broo-hoo-lah
Deck	La cubierta	koo-bee-er-tah
First mate	El primer oficial	pree-mer-oh-fee-thee-al
Flag	La bandera	ban-deh-rah
Harbour	El puerto	pwer-toh
Hatch	La escotilla	es-koh-tee-yah
Headland	La punta	poon-tah
Hook	El anzuelo	an-thweh-loh
Hull	El casco	kas-koh

Learn Spanish In One Week

English	Spanish	Pronunciation
Keel	La quilla	kee-yah
Lifeboat	El bote salvavidas	boh-teh-sal-bah-bee-das
Life jacket	El chaleco salvavidas	chah-leh-koh-sal-bah-bee-das
Mast	El mástil	mas-teel
Mermaid	La sirena	see-reh-nah
Motor / Engine	El motor	moh-tor
Port (left) / Port side	El babor	bah-bor
Port	El puerto	pwer-toh
Propeller	La hélice	eh-lee-theh
Rocks	Las piedras	pee-eh-dras
Rope	El cabo	kah-boh
Rope	La soga	soh-gah
Rudder	El timón	tee-mon
Sailor	El marinero	mah-ree-neh-roh
Sails	Los veleros	beh-leh-rohs
Shipwreck	El naufragio	now-frah-hee-oh
Starboard	El estribor	es-tree-bor
Stern	La popa	poh-pah
Tide	La marea	mah-reh-ah
Wave	La ola	oh-lah

Learn Spanish In One Week

Signs

English	Spanish	Pronunciation
Asbestos	Asbesto	As-bes-toh
Attention	Attención	ah-ten-thee-on
Bargin	Chollo	choh-yoh
Bargain	Ganga	gan-gah
Beware of the dog	Cuidado con el perro	kwee-dah-doh-kon-el-peh-rroh
Beware of the forklift truck	Cuidado con el montacargas	kwee-dah-doh-kon-el-mon-tah-kar-gas
Bus. Stop	Parada	pah-rah-dah
Busy	Ocupado	oh-koo-pah-doh
Caution / Careful	Cuidado	kwee-dah-doh
Caution / Precaution	Precaución	preh-kow-thee-on
Children playing	Niños jugando	nee-nyos-hoo-gan-doh
Close the door slowly	Cierra la puerta lentamente	thee-eh-rah-la-pwer-tah-len-tah-men-teh
Close the gate	Cierra el portón	ther-rah-el-por-ton
Closed	Cerrado	theh-rrah-doh
Cul de sac	Calle sin salida	kah-yeh-seen-sah-lee-dah
Danger	Peligro	peh-lee-groh
Dangerous	Peligroso	peh-lee-groh-soh
Do not litter	No arrojar basuras	noh-ah-roh-har-bah-soo-ras
Do not pass	No pasar	noh-pah-sar

Learn Spanish In One Week

English	Spanish	Pronunciation
Emergency exit	Salida de emergencia	sah-lee-dah-deh-eh-mer-hen-thee-ah
Entrance	Entrada	en-trah-dah
Exit	Salida	sah-lee-dah
Expiry date	La fecha de caducidad	feh-chah-deh-kah-doo-thee-dad
Flammable liquids	Líquidos inflamables	lee-kee-dos-een-flam-ah-blehs
Fire escape	La escalera de incendios	es-kah-leh-rah-deh-een-th-en-dee-oss
Fire exit	La salida de incendios	sah-lee-dah-deh-een-th-en-dee-oss
Fire extinguisher	Extintor	eks-teen-tor
Floor slippery when wet	Piso resbaladizo cuando está mojado	pee-soh-res-bah-lah-dee-thoh-kwan-doh-es-tah-moh-hah-doh
For rent	Se aquila	seh-ah-kee-lah
For sale	Se vende	seh-ben-deh
Free / Vacant	Libre	lee-breh
Gentlemen	Caballeros	kah-bah-yeh-ros
Give way	Ceda el paso	theh-dah-el-pah-soh
Go straight on	Siga derecho	see-gah-deh-reh-choh
Ladies	Damas	dah-mass
Leave your cart here	Deja aquí su carrito	deh-hah-ah-kee-soo-kah-rree-toh

Learn Spanish In One Week

English	Spanish	Pronunciation
No brochures allowed	No se permiten folletos	noh-seh-per-mee-ten-foh-yeh-tos
No cyclists	No ciclistas	noh-thee-clee-stas
No diving	No clavados	noh-klah-bah-dos
No diving	No bucear	noh-boo-theh-ar
No entry	No entrar	noh-en-trar
No exit	No hay salida	noh-eye-sah-lee-dah
No lorries / trucks	No camiones	noh-kah-mee-oh-nehs
Notice / Warning	Aviso	ah-bee-soh
No parking	Prohibido estacionarse	proh-ee-bee-doh-es-tah-thee-on-ar-seh
No smoking	No fumar	noh-foo-mar
No smoking	Prohibido fumar	proh-ee-bee-doh-foo-mar
No smoking area	Sección de no fumar	sek-thee-on-deh-noh-foo-mar
No stopping / Don't stop	No pare	noh-pah-reh
No swimming	No se permite nadar	noh-seh-per-mee-teh-nah-dar
Not for public use	No para uso publico	noh-pah-rah-oo-soh-poo-blee-koh
Open	Abierto	ah-bee-er-toh
Opening hours	Horario de atención	oh-rar-ree-oh-deh-ah-ten-thee-on
Opening hours	Horas de comercio	oh-ras-deh-koh-mer-thee-oh

Learn Spanish In One Week

English	Spanish	Pronunciation
Out of order	Fuera de servicio	fweh-rah-deh-ser-bee-thee-oh
Out of order	No funciona	noh-foon-thee-oh-nah
Private	Privado	pree-bah-doh
Push	Empujar	em-poo-har
Reduced	Reducido	reh-doo-thee-doh
Reserved for	Reservado. para	reh-ser-bah-doh-pah-rah
Sales	Rebajas	reh-bah-has
Sale / Clearance	Liquidación	lee-kee-dah-thee-on
Silence	Silencio	see-len-thee-oh
Smoking area	Sección de fumar	sek-thee-on-deh-foo-mar
Stop	Alto	al-toh
Stop	Pare	pah-reh
Think	Piense	pee-en-seh
Toilets	Aseos	ah-seh-ohs
Trash only	Basura solamente	bah-soo-rah-soh-lah-men-teh
Use other door	Usar otra puerta	oo-sar-oh-trah-pwer-tah
Warning	Advertencia	ad-ber-ten-thee-ah
Wash your hands	Lavarse las manos	lah-bar-seh-las-mah-nos
Welcome	Bienvenido	bee-en-beh-nee-doh
Wet floor	Piso mojado	pee-soh-moh-hah-doh

Learn Spanish In One Week

Shops

English	Spanish	Pronunciation
Baker's shop	La panadería	pah-nah-deh-ree-ah
Bank	El banco	ban-koh
Barber shop	La barbería	bar-beh-ree-ah
Beauty salon	El salón de belleza	sah-lon-deh-beh-yeh-thah
Bookstore	La librería	lee-breh-ree-ah
Butcher's shop	La carnicería	kar-nee-theh-ree-ah
Café	El café	kah-feh
Clothes shop	La tienda de ropa	tee-en-dah-deh-roh-pah
Computer store	La tienda de computadoras	tee-en-dah-deh-kom-poo-tah-doh-ras
Computer store	La tienda de informática	tee-en-dah-deh-een-for-mah-tee-kah
Department store	La tienda por departamentos	tee-en-dah-por-deh-par-tah-men-tos
Dry cleaners	La tintorería	teen-toh-reh-ree-ah
Fish shop	La pescadería	pes-kah-deh-ree-ah
Furniture store	La mueblería	moo-eh-bleh-ree-ah
Garden centre	La tienda de jardinería	tee-en-dah-deh-har-dee-neh-ree-ah
Garden centre	El vivero	bee-beh-roh
General store	La tienda	tee-en-dah
Gift shop	La tienda de regalos	tee-en-dah-deh-reh-gah-lohs

Learn Spanish In One Week

English	Spanish	Pronunciation
Greengrocer's	La verdulería	ber-doo-leh-ree-ah
Hairdresser's	La peluquería	peh-loo-keh-ree-ah
Hypermarket	El hipermercado	ee-per-mer-kah-doh
Jewelry store	La joyería	hoh-yeh-ree-ah
Kiosk	El quiosco	kee-oss-koh
Launderette	La lavandería automática	lah-ban-deh-ree-ah-ow-toh-mah-tee-kah
Music shop	La tienda de música	tee-en-dah-deh-moo-see-kah
Newspaper kiosk	El quiosco de periódicos	kee-os-koh-deh-peh-ree-oh-dee-kos
Pet shop	La tienda de animales	tee-en-dah-deh-ah-nee-mah-lehs
Pharmacy	La farmacia	far-mah-thee-ah
Post office	La oficina de correos	oh-fee-thee-nah-deh-koh-reh-ohs
Restaurant	El restaurante	rres-tow-ran-teh
Sports store	La tienda de deportes	tee-en-dah-deh-deh-por-tehs
Supermarket	El supermercado	soo-per mer-kah-doh
Sweet shop	La dulcería	dool-theh-ree-ah
Tobacco stand	Tabaquería	tah-bah-keh-ree-ah
Tailor shop	La sastrería	sas-treh-ree-ah
Tattoo shop	Estudio de tatuajes	es-too-dee-oh-deh-tah-too-ah-hehs
Travel agency	La agencia de viajes	ah-hen-thee-ah-deh-bee-ah-hehs

Learn Spanish In One Week

Sports

English	Spanish	Pronunciation
Abseiling	El rapel	rrah-pel
American football	El fútbol americano	foot-bol-ah-meh-ree-kah-noh
Archery	El tiro con arco	tee-roh-kon-ar-koh
Badminton	El bádminton	bad-meen-ton
Bowling	Los bolos	boh-los
Boxing	El boxeo	bok-seh-oh
Bridge	El bridge	breech
Canoeing	El piragüismo	pee-rah-gwees-moh
Curling	Curling	koor-leen
Fencing	La esgrima	es-gree-mah
Flying	Volador	boh-lah-dor
Gymnastics	La gimnasia	heem-nah-see-ah
Hang gliding	El aladeltismo	ah-lah-del-tees-moh
Hiking	Excursionismo	eks-koor-see-oh-nees-moh
Horse racing	Las carreras de caballos	kah-rreh-ras-deh-cah-bah-yoss
Hockey	El hockey	hoh-kee
Ice hockey	El hockey sobre hielo	hoh-kee-soh-breh-yeh-loh
Ice skating	El patinaje sobre hielo	pah-tee-nah-heh-soh-breh-yeh-loh
Judo	El yudo	yoo-doh

Learn Spanish In One Week

English	Spanish	Pronunciation
Jujitsu	El jiu-jitsu	hyoo-heet-soo
Karate	Karate	kah-rah-teh
Kickboxing	El kickboxing	keek-bok-seeng
Lacrosse	El lacrosse	lah-kros-seh
Mountaineering	El montañismo	mon-tah-nyees-moh
Netball	Netball	net-bal
Parachuting	El paracaidismo	pah-rah-keye-dees-moh
Paragliding	El parapente	pah-rah-pen-teh
Parasailing	El parasail	pah-rah-sah-eel
Poker	El póquer	poh-ker
Rock climbing	La escalada en roca	es-kah-lah-dah-en-roh-kah
Skateboarding	Andar en monopatín	an-dar-en-moh-noh-pah-teen
Sumo wrestling	Sumo	soo-moh
Table tennis	El tenis de mesa	teh-nees-deh-meh-sah
Trampolining	La gimnasia en trampolín	heem-nah-see-ah-en-tram-poh-leen
Water skiing	El esqui acuático	es-kee-ah-kwah-tee-koh
Weight training	El entrenamiento con pesas	en-treh-nah-mee-en-toh-kon-peh-sas
Windsurfing	El windsurf	ween-surf
Wrestling	La lucha libre	loo-chah-lee-breh

Learn Spanish In One Week

Taxi

English	Spanish	Pronunciation
A receipt please	Un recibo por favor	oon-reh-thee-boh-por-fah-bor
Are we almost there?	¿Estamos casi allí?	es-tah-mos-kah-see-ah-yee
Can you go faster?	¿Puede ir más rápido?	pweh-deh-eer-mas-rah-pee-doh
Can you go slower?	¿Puede ir más despacio?	pweh-deh-eer-mas-des-pah-thee-oh
Do you have any luggage?	¿Tiene equipaje?	tee-eh-neh-eh-kee-pah-heh
Do you have change?	¿Tienes cambio?	tee-en-ehs-kam-bee-oh
How much do I owe you?	¿Cuánto te debo?	kwan-toh-teh-deh-boh
How much will it cost?	¿Cuánto cuesta?	kwan-toh-kweh-stah
I'd like to go	Quisiera ir a	kee-see-eh-rah-eer-ah
I'm in a hurry	Tengo prisa	ten-goh-pree-sah
I'm late	llego tarde	yeh-goh-tar-deh
It's near here	Está cerca de aquí	es-tah-ther-kah-deh-ah-kee
I want to go	Quiero ir	kee-eh-roh-eer
I want to go to the beach	Quiero ir a la playa	kee-eh-roh-eer-ah-lah-plah-yah
Keep the change	Quédese con el cambio	keh-deh-seh-kon-el-kam-bee-oh
No way!	Ni hablar	nee-ab-lar
Not at all	Para nada	pah-rah-nah-dah

Learn Spanish In One Week

English	Spanish	Pronunciation
One minute	Un minuto	oon-mee-noo-toh
Stop here	Para aquí	pah-rah-ah-kee
Take me to this address	llevarme a esta dirección	yev-ar-meh-ah-es-tah-dee-rek-thee-on
The beach please	La playa por favor	lah-plah-yah-por-fah-bor
Too much!	Demasiado	deh-mah-see-ah-doh
To the airport	Al aeropuerto	al-eh-roh-pwer-toh
To the cathedral	A la catedral	ah-lah-kah-teh-dral
To the centre	Al centro	al-th-en-troh
To the cinema	Al cine	al-thee-neh
To the park	Al parque	al-par-keh
To the restaurant	Al restaurante	al-res-tow-ran-teh
To the station	A la estación	ah-lah-es-tah-thee-on
To the theatre	Al teatro	al-teh-ah-troh
Two minutes	Dos minutos	dos-mee-noo-tos
Wait here	Espere aquí	es-peh-reh-ah-kee
We are close	Estamos cerca	es-tah-mos-ther-kah
Yes sir	Sí señor	see-seh-nyor
You are free, aren't you?	¿Está libre, no?	es-tah-lee-breh-noh

Learn Spanish In One Week

Time

English	Spanish	Pronunciation
After	Después de	de-pwes-deh
Again	Otra vez	oh-trah-beth
Ago	Hace	ah-theh
Almost never	Casi nunca	kah-see-noon-kah
Always	Siempre	see-em-preh
Approximately	Aproximadamente	ah-prok-see-mah-dah-men-teh
Around / At about	A eso de	ah-eh-soh-deh
At one o'clock	A la una	ah-lah-oo-nah
At two o'clock	A las dos	ah-las-dos
At night	Por la noche	por-lah-noh-cheh
At the beginning	Al principio	al-preen-thee-pee-oh
At the start	Al comienzo	al-koh-mee-en-thoh
At the start	Al principio	al-preen-thee-pee-oh
At the end of	A finales de	ah-fee-nah-lehs-deh
At the end of July	A finales de julio	ah-fee-nah-lehs-deh-hoo-lee-oh
At the same time	Al mismo tiempo	al-mees-moh-tee-em-poh
At the moment	De momento	deh-moh-men-toh
At this moment	En este momento	en-es-teh-moh-men-toh
At what time?	¿A qué hora?	ah-keh-oh-rah
Autumn	El otoño	oh-toh-nyoh

Learn Spanish In One Week

English	Spanish	Pronunciation
Before	Antes	an-tehs
Daily	Diario	dee-ah-ree-oh
Day	El día	dee-ah
Day after tomorrow	Pasado mañana	pah-sah-doh-man-yah-nah
Day before yesterday	Anteayer	an-teh-ah-yer
Days of the week	Los días de la semana	dee-ass-deh-lah-seh-mah-nah
During	Durante	doo-ran-teh
Early	Temprano	tem-prah-noh
Evening	La tarde	tar-deh
Every day	Cada día	kah-dah-dee-ah
Every day	Todos los días	toh-dos-los-dee-ass
Exactly	Exactamente	ek-sak-tah-men-teh
Final / Last	Último	ool-tee-moh
Finally	Finalmente	fee-nal-men-teh
Five past	Y cinco	ee-theen-koh
Five to	Menos cinco	meh-nos-theen-koh
From	A partir de	ah-par-teer-deh
From time to time	De vez en cuando	deh-beth-en-kwan-doh
Fortnight	La quincena	keen-theh-nah
Fortnight	Quince días	keen-theh-dee-ass

Learn Spanish In One Week

English	Spanish	Pronunciation
Half an hour	Media hora	meh-dee-ah-oh-rah
Half past	Y media	ee-meh-dee-ah
Hour	La hora	oh-rah
In the afternoon	De la tarde	deh-lah-tar-deh
In the morning	De la mañana	deh-lah-man-yah-nah
In the morning	Por la mañana	por-lah-man-yah-nah
In the night	De la noche	deh-lah-noh-cheh
I'll talk to you later	Te hablo más tarde	teh-ah-bloh-mass-tar-deh
It's five past ten	Son las diez y cinco	son-las-dee-eth-ee-theen-koh
It's one thirty	Es la una y media	es-lah-oo-nah-ee-meh-dee-ah
It's quarter past seven	Son las siete y cuarto	son-las-see-eh-teh-ee-kwar-toh
It's twelve minutes past three	Son las tres y doce	son-las-tres-ee-doh-theh
It's two o'clock exactly	Son las dos en punto	son-las-dos-en-poon-toh
Just now	Ahora mismo	ah-oh-rah-mees-moh
Last	Pasado/a	pah-sah-doh / dah
Last night	Anoche	ah-noh-cheh
Last year	Año pasado	ah-nyoh-pah-sah-doh
Late	Tarde	tar-deh
Later	Más tarde	mass-tar-deh

Learn Spanish In One Week

English	Spanish	Pronunciation
Midday	El mediodía	meh-dee-oh-dee-ah
Midnight	La medianoche	meh-dee-ah-noh-cheh
Minute	El minuto	mee-noo-toh
Month	El mes	mess
Morning	La mañana	man-yah-nah
Nearly	Casi	kah-see
Never	Nunca	noon-kah
Never ever	Jamás	hah-mas
Next	Próximo	prok-see-moh
Next	Siguiente	see-gee-en-teh
Night	La noche	noh-cheh
Noon	Mediodía	meh-dee-oh-dee-ah
Now	Ahora	ah-oh-rah
Often	A menudo	ah-meh-noo-doh
On the dot	En punto	en-poon-toh
On time	A tiempo	ah-tee-em-poh
On time	Puntual	poon-twal
Party	La fiesta	fee-es-tah
Past	El pasado	pah-sah-doh
Quarter past	Y cuarto	ee-kwar-toh

Learn Spanish In One Week

English	Spanish	Pronunciation
Quarter to	Menos cuarto	meh-noss-kwar-toh
Seasons	Las estaciónes	es-tah-thee-on-ehs
Second	El segundo	seh-goon-doh
Since / From	Desde	des-deh
Sometimes	A veces	ah-beh-thehs
Sometimes	Algunas veces	al-goo-nas-beh-thehs
Soon	Pronto	pron-toh
Spring	La primavera	pree-mah-beh-rah
Straight away	Ahora mismo	ah-oh-rah-mees-moh
Straight away / Immediately	Enseguida	en-seh-gee-dah
Suddenly	De repente	deh-rreh-pen-teh
Summer	El verano	beh-rah-noh
Ten past	Y diez	ee-dee-eth
Ten to	Menos diez	meh-nos-dee-eth
The day after tomorrow	Pasado mañana	pah-sah-doh-man-yah-nah
The hour	La hora	oh-rah
The next day	Al día siguiente	al-dee-ah-see-gee-en-teh
The timetable	El horario	oh-rah-ree-oh

Learn Spanish In One Week

English	Spanish	Pronunciation
Tomorrow	Mañana	man-yah-nah
The weekend	El fin de semana	el-feen-deh-seh-mah-nah
The working day	El día laboral	el-dee-ah-lah-boh-ral
Then	Entonces	en-ton-thehs
This night	Esta noche	es-tah-noh-cheh
This year	Este año	es-teh-ah-nyoh
Today	Hoy	oy
Twenty past	Y veinte	ee-bayn-teh
Twenty five past	Y veintecinco	ee-bayn-teh-theen-koh
Weekend	Fin de semana	feen-deh-seh-mah-nah
What time are you coming?	¿A qué hora vienes?	ah-keh-oh-rah-bee-eh-nes
What time are we leaving?	¿A qué hora nos vamos?	ah-keh-oh-rah-nos-bah-moss
What time is it?	¿A qué hora es?	ah-keh-oh-rah-es
What time is the movie?	¿A qué hora es la película?	ah-keh-oh-rah-es-lah-peh-lee-koo-lah
Winter	El invierno	een-bee-er-noh
Year	El año	ah-nyoh
Yesterday	Ayer	ah-yer
Yesterday morning	Ayer por la mañana	ah-yer-por-lah-man-yah-nah

Learn Spanish In One Week

Tools

English	Spanish	Pronunciation
Ax / Hatchet	Él hacha	ah-chah
Chisel	El cincel	theen-thel
Clamp	La abrazadera	ah-brah-thah-deh-rah
Drill	El taladro	tah-lah-droh
Drill bit	La broca	broh-kah
Hammer	El martillo	mar-tee-yoh
Hacksaw	La sierra para metales	see-eh-rah-pah-rah-meh-tah-lehs
Machete	El machete	mah-cheh-tah
Nails	Los clavos	klah-bos
Pliers	Los alicates	ah-lee-kah-tehs
Ruler	La regla	rreh-glah
Saw	La sierra	see-eh-rrah
Screwdriver	El destornillador	des-tor-nee-yah-dor
Screws	Los tornillos	tor-nee-yohs
Spanner	La llave de tubo	yah-beh-deh-too-boh
Spanner	La llave inglesa	yah-beh-eeng-leh-sah
Swiss army knife	La navaja suiza	nah-bah-hah-swee-thah
Tape measure	La cinta métrica	theen-tah-meh-tree-kah
Toolbox	La caja de herramientas	kah-hah-deh-eh-rrah-mee-en-tas

Learn Spanish In One Week

Train

English	Spanish	Pronunciation
Arrival	La entrada	en-trah-dah
Arrival	La llegada	yeh-gah-dah
A ticket to	Un billete para	oon-bee-yeh-teh-pah-rah
Cancellation	La anulación	ah-noo-lah-thee-on
Cancellation	La cancelación	kan-seh-al-thee-on
Compartment	El compartimiento	kom-par-tee-mee-en-toh
Conductor	El cobrador	koh-brah-dor
Direct train	Tren directo	tren-dee-rek-toh
First class	La primera clase	pree-meh-rah-klah-seh
How many people?	¿Cuántas personas?	kwan-tass-per-soh-nas
I'm in a hurry	Tengo prisa	ten-goh-pree-sah
Information	La información	een-for-mah-thee-on
It's for two people	Es para dos personas	es-pah-rah-dos-per-soh-nas
Left luggage	La consigna	kon-seeg-nah
Journey	El viaje	bee-ah-heh
On time	A tiempo	ah-tee-em-poh
One way ticket	Un billete de ida	bee-yeh-teh-deh-ee-dah
Open return	Vuelta abierta	bwel-tah-ah-bee-er-tah
Passenger	El pasajero	pah-sah-heh-roh
Platform	El andén	an-den

Learn Spanish In One Week

English	Spanish	Pronunciation
Railway tracks	Las vías del tren	las bee ass del-tren
Refund	El reembolso	reh-em-bol-soh
Return journey	Viaje de vuelta	bee-ah-heh-deh-bwel-tah
Return ticket	Un billete de ida y vuelta	oon-bee-yeh-teh-deh-ee-dah-ee-bwel-tah
Seat	El asiento	ah-see-en-toh
Second class	La segunda clase	seh-goon-dah-klah-seh
Second class	Turista	too-rees-tah
Strike	La huelga	wel-gah
The next train	El próximo	tren
There is a delay	Hay un retraso	eye-oon-reh-trah-soh
Ticket	El billete	bee-yeh-teh
Ticket office	La taquilla	tah-kee-yah
Time table / Schedule	La horario	oh-rah-ree-oh
Track	La vía	bee-ah
Train station	Estación	es-tah-thee-on
Train station	La estación de tren	es-tah-thee-on-deh-tren
Underpass	El paso subterráneo	pah-soh-soob-teh-rrah-nee-oh
Waiting room	La sala de espera	sah-lah-deh-es-peh-rah
When does the train leave?	¿Cuándo sale el tren	kwan-doh-sah-leh-el-tren

Learn Spanish In One Week

Transport and Vehicles

English	Spanish	Pronunciation
Bicycle	La bicicleta	bee-thee-kleh-tah
Boat	El bote	boh-teh
Bus	El autobús	ow-toh-boos
Canoe	La canoa	kah-noh-ah
Car	El coche	koh-cheh
Cruise ship	Él crucero	kroo-theh-roh
Ferry	El ferry	feh-ree
Ferry boat	El transbordador	trans-bor-dah-dor
Helicopter	El helicóptero	eh-lee-kop-teh-roh
Hot-air ballon	El globo aerostático	gloh-boh-eh-roh-stah-tee-koh
Light aircraft	La avioneta	ah-bee-oh-neh-tah
Limousine	La limusina	lee-moo-see-nah
Lorry	El camión	kah-mee-on
Motorcycle	Motocicleta	moh-toh-thee-kleh-tah
Pickup truck	La camioneta	kah-mee-oh-neh-tah
Plane	El avión	ah-bee-on
Ship	El barco	bar-koh
Taxi	El taxi	tak-see
Train	El tren	tren
Tram	El tranvía	tran-bee-ah

Learn Spanish In One Week

Vegetables

English	Spanish	Pronunciation
Asparagus	El espárrago	es-pah-rrah-goh
Avocado	El aguacate	ah-gwah-kah-teh
Bean	El frijol	free-hol
Bean	La habichuela	ah-bee-choo-eh-lah
Bean	La judía	hoo-dee-ah
Beets	Las remolachas	rreh-moh-lah-chah
Broad bean	La haba	ah-bah
Broccoli	El brócoli	broh-koh-lee
Brussels sprout	La col de bruselas	la-kol-deh-broo-seh-las
Cabbage	El repollo	reh-poh-yoh
Cabbage	La col	kol
Carrot	La zanahoria	tha-nah-oh-ree-ah
Cauliflower	La coliflor	koh-lee-flor
Celery	El apio	ah-pee-oh
Corn	El maíz	mah-eeth
Cucumber	El pepino	peh-pee-noh
Eggplant	La berenjena	beh-ren-heh-nah
Garlic	El ajo	ah-hoh
Ginger	El jengibre	hen-hee-breh
Green beans	Las judías verdes	hoo-dee-ass-ber-dehs

Learn Spanish In One Week

English	Spanish	Pronunciation
Jalapeño	Jalapeño	ha-lah-peh-nyoh
Kale	La col rizada	kol-ree-thah-dah
Leek	El puerro	pweh-rroh
Kale	La col rizada	kol-ree-thah-dah
Leek	El puerro	pweh-rroh
Lettuce	La lechuga	leh-choo-gah
Mushroom	La seta	seh-tah
Onion	La cebolla	theh-boh-yah
Pea	El guisante	gee-san-teh
Peppers	Los pimientos	pee-mee-en-tos
Potato	La patata	pah-tah-tah
Pumpkin	La calabaza	kah-lah-bah-thah
Radish	El rábano	rrah-bah-noh
Rhubarb	El ruibarbo	roo-ee-bar-boh
Spinach	La espinaca	es-pee-nah-kah
Squash	La calabaza	kah-lah-bah-thah
Sweet potato	La batata	bah-tah-tah
Tomato	El tomate	toh-mah-teh
Turnip	El nabo	nah-noh
Watercress	El berro	beh-rroh

Learn Spanish In One Week

Verbs

English	Spanish	Pronunciation
Buy / To buy	Comprar	kom-prah
I buy	Yo compro	joh-kom-proh
I bought	Compré	kom-preh
I want to buy	Quiero comprar	kee-eh-roh-kom-prah
I would like to buy	Me gustaría comprar	meh-goos-tah-ree-ah-kom-prar
I bought you	Te compré	teh-kom-preh
I bought for you	Yo compré para tí	joh-kom-preh-pah-rah-tee
I should buy	Yo debería comprar	joh-deh-beh-ree-ah-kom-prar
I can buy	Puedo comprar	pweh-doh-kom-prar
I could buy	Yo podría comprar	joh-poh-dree-ah-kom-prar
I like to buy	Me gusta comprar	meh-goos-tah-kom-prar
I have been buying	He estado comprando	eh-es-tah-doh-kom-pran-doh
I will buy	Yo compraré	joh-kom-prah-reh
To accept	Aceptar	ah-thep-tar
To accompany	Acompañar	ah-kom-pah-nyar
To add	Añadir	ah-nyah-deer
To advise	Aconsejar	ah-kon-seh-har
To allow	Permitir	per-mee-teer
To answer	Contestar	kon-tes-tar

Learn Spanish In One Week

English	Spanish	Pronunciation
To appear / To show up	Aparecer	ah-pah-reh-ther
To apply	Aplicar	ah-plee-kar
To argue	Discutir	dees-koo-teer
To arrive, come, reach	llegar	yeh-gar
To ask	Preguntar	preh-goon-tar
To ask a question	Hacer una pregunta	ah-ther-oo-nah-preh-goon-tah
To ask for	Pedir	peh-deer
To avoid	Evitar	eh-bee-tar
To bath / To bathe	Bañarse	bah-nyar-seh
To be	Estar	es-tar
To be	Ser	ser
To be able / can	Poder	poh-der
To be born	Nacer	nah-ther
To be called	llamarse	yah-mar-seh
To be careful	Tener cuidado	teh-ner-kwee-dah-doh
To be cold	Tener frío	teh-ner-free-oh
To be hot	Tener calor	teh-ner-kah-lor
To be hungry	Tener hambre	teh-ner-am-breh
To be in a hurry	Tener prisa	teh-ner-pree-sah
To be interested in	Interesarse en	een-teh-reh-sar-seh-en

Learn Spanish In One Week

English	Spanish	Pronunciation
To be keen to / To feel like	Tener ganas de	teh-ner-gah-nas-deh
To be lucky	Tener suerte	teh-ner-swer-teh
To be missing	Faltar	fal-tar
To be sleepy / tired	Tener sueño	teh-ner-sweh-nyoh
To be sorry	Lamentar	lah-men-tar
To be sorry	Sentir	sen-teer
To be successful	Tener éxito	teh-ner-ek-see-toh
To be thirsty	Tener sed	teh-ner-sed
To begin	Empezar	em-peh-thar
To believe	Creer	kreh-er
To borrow	Pedir prestado	peh-deer-preh-stah-doh
To break	Romper	rrom-per
To bring	Traer	trah-er
To brush (teeth / hair)	Cepillarse	theh-pee-yar-seh
To buy	Comprar	kom-prar
To buy tickets (for a show)	Sacar entradas	sah-kar-en-trah-das
To calculate	Calcular	kal-koo-lar
To call	llamar	yah-mar
To carry / To bring	llevar	yeh-bar

Learn Spanish In One Week

English	Spanish	Pronunciation
To change	Cambiar	kam-bee-ar
To change (trains etc)	Hacer transbordo	ah-ther-trans-bor-doh
To chat	Charlar	char-lar
To check / To find out	Averiguar	ah-beh-ree-gwar
To check / To verify	Verificar	beh-ree-fee-kar
To choose	Elegir	eh-leh-heer
To clear the table	Quitar la mesa	kee-tah-lah-meh-sah
To click	Cliquear	klee-keh-ar
To climb / To go up	Subir	soo-beer
To climb mountains	Escalar montañas	es-kah-lar-mon-tah-nyas
To close	Cerrar	theh-rrah
To collide / To crash	Chocar	choh-kar
To come	Venir	beh-neer
To complain	Quejarse	keh-har-seh
To contact	Contactar	kon-tak-tar
To continue	Continuar	kon-tee-nwar
To copy	Copiar	koh-pee-ar
To correct	Corregir	koh-rreh-heer
To cost	Costar	kos-tar
To count	Contar	kon-tar

Learn Spanish In One Week

English	Spanish	Pronunciation
To cry	llorar	yoh-rar
To dance	Bailar	beye-lar
To decide	Decidir	deh-thee-deer
To describe	Describir	des-kree-beer
To deserve	Merecer	meh-reh-ther
To die	Morir	moh-reer
To discuss	Discutir	dees-koo-teer
To dismiss	Despedir	des-peh-deer
To do the vacuum cleaning	Pasar la aspiradora	pah-sar-lah-as-pee-rah-doh-rah
To do the washing up	Fregar los platos	freh-gar-los-plah-tos
To do / To make	Hacer	ah-ther
To download (music)	Descargar (música)	des-kar-gar (moo-see-kah)
To draw	Dibujar	dee-boo-har
To drink	Beber	beh-ber
To drive	Conducir	kon-doo-theer
To eat	Comer	koh-mer
To end	Terminar	ter-mee-nar
To enjoy oneself	Divertirse	dee-ber-teer-seh
To enter	Entrar	en-trar

Learn Spanish In One Week

English	Spanish	Pronunciation
To escape	Escaparse	es-kah-par-seh
To exist	Existir	ek-see-teer
To fail	Fallar	fah-yar
To fail (an exam)	Suspender (un examen)	soos-pen-der (oon-ek-sah-men)
To fall	Caer	kah-er
To feel / To regret	Sentir	sen-reer
To fill	llenar	yeh-nar
To fill out (a form)	Rellenar	reh-yeh-nar
To find / To meet	Encontrar	en-kon-trar
To finish / To end	Acabar	ah-kah-bar
To finish / To end	Terminar	ter-mee-nar
To follow	Seguir	seh-geer
To forget	Olvidar	ol-bee-dar
To forgive	Perdonar	per-doh-nar
To get / To obtain	Conseguir	kon-seh-geer
To get good marks	Sacar buenas notas	sah-kar-bweh-nas-noh-tas
To get angry	Enfadarse	en-fah-dar-seh
To get dressed	Vestirse	bes-teer-seh
To get off (bus / train)	Bajar	bah-har
To get on well with	llevarse bien con	yeh-bar-seh-bee-en-kon

Learn Spanish In One Week

English	Spanish	Pronunciation
To get up	Levantarse	leh-ban-tar-seh
To give	Dar	dar
To give (presents)	Ofrecer / Dar (regalos) regalar	oh-freh-ther / dar (reh-gah-los) reh-gah-lar
To give orders	Mandar	man-dar
To go	Ir	eer
To go along (in a car)	Circular / Viajar (en coche)	theer-koo-lar / bee-ah-har (en-koh-cheh)
To go down	Bajar	bah-har
To go for a walk	Dar un paseo	dar-oon-pah-seh-oh
To go for a walk	Ir de paseo	eer-deh-pah-seh-oh
To go to bed	Acostarse	ah-koh-star-seh
To go shopping	Ir de compras	eer-deh-kom-pras
To go up	Subir	soo-beer
To hand over	Entregar	en-treh-gar
To hate	Odiar	oh-dee-ar
To have	Tener	teh-ner
To have	Haber	ah-ber
To have breakfast	Desayunar	des-ah-yoo-nar
To have a cold	Estar resfriado	es-tar-res-free-ah-doh
To have dinner	Cenar	theh-nar

Learn Spanish In One Week

English	Spanish	Pronunciation
To have lunch	Almorzar	al-mor-thar
To have to	Tener que	teh-ner-keh
To hear	Oír	oh-eer
To help	Ayudar	ah-yoo-dar
To hope	Esperar	es-peh-rar
To hurry	Darse prisa	dar-seh-pree-sah
To hurt (emotionally)	Doler	doh-ler
To imagine	Imaginar	ee-mah-hee-nar
To improve	Mejorar	meh-hoh-rar
To inform	Informar	een-for-mar
To introduce	Introducir	een-troh-doo-theer
To invite	Invitar	een-bee-tar
To iron / To press	Planchar	plan-char
To jump	Saltar	sal-tar
To know (people / places)	Conocer	koh-noh-ther
To know (information)	Saber	sah-ber
To land	Aterrizar	ah-teh-rree-thar
To last	Durar	doo-rar
To laugh	Reír	reh-eer

Learn Spanish In One Week

English	Spanish	Pronunciation
To lay the table	Poner la mesa	poh-ner-lah-meh-sah
To learn	Aprender	ah-pren-der
To leave / Go away	Marcharse	mar-char-seh
To leave (an object)	Dejar	deh-har
To leave / To depart	Salir	sah-leer
To lend	Prestar	pres-tar
To light	Encender	en-th-en-der
To like	Gustar	goos-tar
To listen	Escuchar	es-koo-char
To live	Vivir	bee-beer
To load / To charge	Cargar	kar-gar
To look after	Cuidar	kwee-dar
To look for	Buscar	boos-kar
To look like / To resemble	Parecerse a	pah-reh-ther-seh-ah
To lose	Perder	per-der
To love	Amar	ah-mar
To love	Querer	keh-rer
To love (to like strongly)	Encantar	en-kan-tar
To make	Hacer	ah-ther

Learn Spanish In One Week

English	Spanish	Pronunciation
To make a mistake	Equivocarse	eh-kee-boh-kar-seh
To manage / Direct or Run	Dirigir	dee-ree-heer
To meet	Conocer	koh-noh-ther
To meet	Encontrarse	en-kon-trar-seh
To miss	Echar de menos	eh-char-deh-meh-nos
To need	Necesitar	neh-theh-see-tar
To note / To observe	Notar	noh-tar
To occur / To happen	Ocurrir	oh-koo-rreer
To open	Abrir	ah-breer
To order / to ask for	Pedir	peh-deer
To organise	Organizar	or-gah-nee-thar
To owe	Deber	deh-ber
To park	Aparcar	ah-par-kar
To pass (exam)	Aprobar (un examen)	ah-proh-bar (oon-ek-sah-men)
To pass / To spend time	Pasar	pah-sar
To permit / To allow	Permitir	per-mee-teer
To phone	Telefonear	teh-leh-foh-neh-ar
To play (game / sport)	Jugar	hoo-gar
To play (musical instrument)	Tocar	toh-kar

Learn Spanish In One Week

English	Spanish	Pronunciation
To please	Gustar	goos-tar
To practise	Practicar	prak-tee-kar
To prefer	Preferir	preh-feh-reer
To present / To introduce	Presentar	preh-sen-tar
To prevent / To warn	Prevenir	preh-beh-neer
To produce	Producir	proh-doo-theer
To pull	Tirar	tee-rar
To push	Empujar	em-poo-har
To put / To place	Poner	poh-ner
To put back / To replace	Reemplazar	reh-em-plah-thar
To put on make up	Maquillarse	mah-kee-yar-seh
To rain	llover	yoh-ber
To read	Leer	leh-er
To realise	Darse cuenta de	dar-seh-kwen-tah-deh
To receive	Recibir	reh-thee-beer
To recommend	Recomendar	reh-koh-men-dar
To refund	Reembolsar	reh-em-bol-sar
To regret	Arrepentirse	ah-rreh-pen-teer-seh
To remember	Recorder	reh-kor-dar

Learn Spanish In One Week

English	Spanish	Pronunciation
To rent / To hire	Alquilar	al-kee-lar
To repair	Reparar	reh-pah-rar
To repeat	Repetir	reh-peh-teer
To replace	Reponer	reh-poh-ner
To reply	Responder	res-pon-der
To request / To ask for	Pedir	peh-deer
To research	Investigar	een-bes-tee-gar
To reserve	Reservar	reh-ser-bar
To return / to go back	Volver	bol-ber
To revise	Repasar	rreh-pah-sar
To ride a horse	Montar a caballo	mon-tar-ah-kah-bah-yoh
To Ring / Call / Phone	llamar	yah-mar
To run	Correr	koh-rrer
To save	Salvar	sal-bar
To save (money)	Ahorrar (dinero)	ah-oh-rar (dee-neh-roh)
To say / To tell	Decir	deh-theer
To say goodbye	Despedirse	des-peh-seer-seh
To sear for / look for	Buscar	boos-kar
To seem / To appear	Parecer	pah-reh-ther
To sell	Vender	ben-der

Learn Spanish In One Week

English	Spanish	Pronunciation
To send	Mandar	man-dar
To serve	Servir	ser-beer
To share	Compartir	kom-par-teer
To shave	Afeitarse	ah-feh-tar-seh
To show	Mostrar	mos-trar
To shower	Ducharse	doo-char-seh
To sign	Firmar	feer-mar
To sing	Cantar	kan-tar
To sit down	Sentarse	sen-tar-seh
To skate	Patinar	pah-tee-nar
To ski	Esquiar	es-kee-ar
To sleep	Dormir	dor-meer
To smile	Sonreír	son-reh-eer
To smoke	Fumar	foo-mar
To speak	Hablar	ah-blar
To spend (money)	Gastar (dinero)	gas-tar (dee-neh-roh)
To spend (time)	Pasar (tiempo)	pah-sar (tee-em-poh)
To start	Empezar	em-peh-thar
To stay / To remain	Quedarse	keh-dar-se
To steal	Robar	rroh-bar

Learn Spanish In One Week

English	Spanish	Pronunciation
To stick	Pegar	peh-gar
To stop	Parar	pah-rar
To study	Estudiar	es-too-dee-ar
To succeed	Lograr	loh-grar
To succeed / To triumph	Triunfar	tree-oon-far
To sunbathe	Tomar el sol	toh-mar-el-sol
To surf the internet	Navegar en internet	nah-beh-gar-en-een-ter-net
To swim	Nadar	nah-dar
To take	Coger	koh-her
To take / To drink	Tomar	toh-mar
To take advantage of	Aprovechar	ah-proh-beh-char
To take out / To stick out	Sacar	sah-kar
To teach	Enseñar	en-seh-nyar
To tell / To recount	Contar	kon-tar
To thank	Agradecer	ah-grah-deh-ther
To think	Pensar	pen-sar
To throw	Tirar	tee-rar
To tidy	Arreglar	ah-rreh-glar
To touch	Tocar	toh-kar
To treat / To handle	Tratar	trah-tar

Learn Spanish In One Week

English	Spanish	Pronunciation
To try	Intentar	een-ten-tar
To try to	Tratar de	trah-tar-deh
To twist / To turn	Torcer	tor-ther
To type	Escribir a máquina	es-kree-beer-ah-mah-kee-nah
To understand	Entender	en-ten-der
To use	Usar	oo-sar
To use	Utilzar	oo-tee-lee-thar
To visit	Visitar	bee-see-tar
To wait for	Esperar	es-peh-rar
To walk	Andar	an-dar
To walk	Caminar	kah-mee-nar
To walk	Pasear	pah-seh-ar
To want	Querer	keh-rer
To wash	Lavar	lah-bar
To wash (oneself)	Lavarse	lah-bar-seh
To watch / To look at	Mirar	mee-rar
To wear	llevar	yeh-bar
To work	Trabajar	trah-bah-har
To work (to function)	Funcionar	foon-thee-oh-nar
To write	Escribir	es-kree-beer

Learn Spanish In One Week

Weather

English	Spanish	Pronunciation
Bad weather	Mal tiempo	mal-tee-em-poh
Bright / Good weather	Buen tiempo	bwen-tee-em-poh
Chilly / Fresh	Fresco/a	fres-koh / kah
Clear	Despejado/a	des-peh-hah-doh / dah
Climate	El clima	klee-mah
Cloud	La nube	noo-beh
Cloudy	Nublado	noo-blah-doh
Cloudy day	El día nublado	dee-ah-noo-blah-doh
Cold	Frío / Fría	free-oh / free-ah
Cold and snowy	Frío y nevoso	free-oh-ee-neh-boh-soh
Cold and windy	Frío y ventoso	free-oh-ee-ben-toh-soh
Cold and windy	Frío y viento	free-oh-ee-bee-en-toh
Degree	El grado	gra-doh
Downpour / Shower	El aguacero	ah-gwah-theh-roh
Downpour / Shower	El chaparrón	chah-pah-rron
Dry	Seco	seh-koh
Fog	La niebla	nee-eh-blah
Foggy	Neblinoso	neh-blee-noh-soh
Forecast	El pronóstico	proh-nos-tee-koh
Good weather	Buen tiempo	bwen-tee-em-poh

Learn Spanish In One Week

English	Spanish	Pronunciation
Hail	El granizo	grah-nee-thoh
Heat	El calor	kah-lor
Heavy shower	El chubasco	choo-bass-koh
Highest temperature	Temperatura más alta	tem-peh-rah-too-rah-mas-al-tah
Hot	Caluroso/a	kah-loo-roh-soh / sah
Humid	Húmedo/a	oo-meh-doh / dah
Ice	El hielo	yeh-loh
In the east	Al este	al-es-teh
In the east	En el este	en-el-es-teh
In the north	Al norte	al-nor-teh
In the north	En el norte	en-el-nor-teh
In the south	Al sur	al-soor
In the south	En el sur	en-el-soor
In the west	Al oeste	al-oh-es-teh
In the west	En el oeste	en-el-oh-es-teh
It is freezing	Está helado	es-tah-eh-lah-doh
It is lightning	Hay relámpagos	eye-reh-lam-pah-gos
It is misty / foggy	Está neblinoso	es-tah-neh-blee-noh-soh
It is raining	Está lloviendo	es-tah-yoh-bee-en-doh
It is snowing	Está nevando	es-tah-neh-ban-doh

Learn Spanish In One Week

English	Spanish	Pronunciation
It is thundering	Hay truenos	eue-troo-eh-nos
Lightning (bolt)	El relámpago	rreh-lam-pah-goh
Lowest temperature	Temperatura mínima	tem-peh-rah-too-rah-mee-nee-mah
Mild	Templado/a	tem-plah-doh / dah
Misty	Neblinoso	neh-blee-noh-soh
Nice weather	Buen tiempo	bwen-tee-em-poh
Overcast	Está nublado	es-tah-noo-blah-doh
Rain	La lluvia	yoo-bee-ah
Rainfall	La lluvia	yoo-bee-ah
Rainy	lluvioso	yoo-bee-oh-soh
Shade	La sombra	som-brah
Shower	El chubasco	choo-bas-koh
Sky	El cielo	thee-eh-loh
Snow	La nieve	nyeh-beh
Stable	Estable	es-tah-bleh
Storm / Thunder storm	La tormenta	tor-men-tah
Stormy / Turbulent	Tormentoso	tor-men-toh-soh
Sun	Él sol	sol
Sunny	Soleado	soh-leh-ah-doh

Learn Spanish In One Week

English	Spanish	Pronunciation
Temperature	La temperatura	tem-peh-rah-too-rah
The sun is shining	Brilla el sol	bree-yah-el-sol
There's fog / foggy	Hay niebla	eye-nee-eh-blah
To brighten up	Alegrar	ah-leh-grar
To change	Cambiar	kam-bee-ar
To freeze	Helar	eh-lar
To hail	Granizar	grah-nee-thar
To improve / get better	Mejorar	meh-hoh-rar
To rain	llover	yoh-ber
To shine	Brillar	bree-yar
To snow	Nevar	neh-bar
Sunny period	Período soleado	peh-ree-oh-doh-soh-leh-ah-doh
Weather	El tiempo	tee-em-poh
Weather forecast	El pronóstico del tiempo	proh-nos-tee-koh-del-tee-em-poh
Weather report	El boletín meteorológico	boh-leh-teen-meh-teh-oh-roh-loh-hee-koh
Wind	El viento	bee-en-toh
Windy	Ventoso	ben-toh-soh

Learn Spanish In One Week

Weights & Measures

English	Spanish	Pronunciation
A little	Un poco	oon-poh-koh
A lot	Mucho	moo-choh
A quater	Un cuarto	kwar-toh
Bag	La bolsa	bol-sah
Big	Grande	gran-deh
Bottle	La botella	boh-yeh-yah
Box	La caja	kah-hah
Can	El bote / La lata	boh-teh / lah-tah
Carton	El cartón	kar-ton
Centimeter	El centímetro	th-en-tee-meh-troh
Double	El doble	doh-bleh
Empty	Vacio/a	bah-thee-oh / ah
Fat	Gordo/a	gor-doh / dah
Full / Complete	Completo	kom-pleh-toh
Full	lleno/a	yeh-noh / nah
Gram	Gramo	grah-moh
Half	Medio	meh-dee-oh
Height	La altura	al-too-rah
Litre	El litro	lee-troh
Low / Short	Bajo	bah-hoh

Learn Spanish In One Week

English	Spanish	Pronunciation
Medium	Mediano	meh-dee-ah-noh
Packet / Package	El paquete	pah-keh-teh
Piece	El pedazo	peh-dah-thoh
Piece / Slice	El trozo	troh-thoh
Portion / Helping	Ración	rrah-thee-on
Quantity	La cantidad	kan-tee-dad
Size	La talla	tah-yah
Sufficient / Enough	Suficiente	soo-fee-thee-en-teh
Tall	Alto	al-toh
The measurement	La medida	meh-dee-dah
The half	La mitad	mee-tad
The weight	El peso	peh-soh
Thick	Grueso	groo-eh-soh
Thin	Delgado	del-gah-doh
Tight / Narrow	Estrecho	es-treh-choh
Tin	La lata	lah-tah
To be enough	Bastar	bas-tar
To measure	Medir	meh-deer
To weigh	Pesar	peh-sar
Wide / baggy	Ancho	an-choh

Learn Spanish In One Week

Work

English	Spanish	Pronunciation
Accountant	El / La contable	kon-tah-bleh
Actor	El actor	ak-tor
Actress	La actriz	ak-treeth
Air hostess	La azafata	ah-thah-fah-tah
Air traffic controller	El controlador aéreo	kon-troh-lah-dor-ah-eh-reh-oh
Archaeologist	El / La arqueólogo	ar-keh-oh-loh-goh
Architect	El / La arquitecto/a	ar-kee-tek-toh / tah
Artist	El / La artista	ar-tees-tah
Attorney	El / La abogado/a	ah-boh-gah-doh/dah
Banker	El / La banquero/a	ban-keh-roh / rah
Barber	El / La barbero/a	bar-beh-roh / rah
Biologist	El / La biólogo/a	bee-oh-loh-goh / gah
Bodyguard	El / La guardaespaldas	gwar-dah-es-pal-das
Bricklayer	El / La albañil	al-bah-nyeel
Builder	El / La albañil	al-bah-nyeel
Butcher	El / La carnicero/a	kar-nee-theh-roh / rah
Bus driver	El / La conductor/a de autobús	kon-dook-tor/a-deh-ow-toh-boos
Carpenter	El / La carpintero/a	kar-peen-teh-roh / rah
Cashier	El / La cajero/a	kah-heh-roh / rah

Learn Spanish In One Week

English	Spanish	Pronunciation
Chauffeur	El / La chófer	choh-fer
Chef	El / La chef	chef
Clown	El / La payaso	pah-yah-soh
Coach	El / La entrenador/a	en-treh-nah-dor/ah
Dancer	El / La bailarín/a	beye-lah-reen/ah
Dental hygienist	El / la higienista dental	ee-hee-en-ee-stah-den-tal
Dentist	El / La dentista	den-tees-tah
Designer	El / La diseñador/a	dee-seh-nyah-dor/ah
Developer	El / La desarrollador/a	des-ah-rroh-yah-dor/ah
Dietitian	El / La nutricionista	noo-tree-thee-oh-nees-tah
Director	El / La director/a	dee-rek-tor/ah
Doctor	El / La doctor/a	dok-tor/ah
Doctor	El / La médico	meh-dee-koh / kah
Economist	El / La economista	eh-koh-noh-mees-tah
Editor	El / La editor/a	eh-dee-tor/ah
Electrician	El / La electricista	eh-lek-tree-thees-tah
Engineer	El / La ingeniero/a	een-heh-nee-eh-roh / rah
Filmmaker	El / La cineasta	thee-neh-as-tah
Fireman / woman	El / la bombero/a	bom-beh-roh / rah
Fisherman	El / La pescador/a	pes-kah-dor/ah

Learn Spanish In One Week

English	Spanish	Pronunciation
Fishmonger	El / La pescadero/a	pes-kah-deh-roh / rah
Footballer	El / La futbolista	foot-boh-lees-tah
Geologist	El / La geólogo/a	heh-oh-loh-goh / gah
Hairdresser	El / La peluquero/a	peh-loo-keh-roh / rah
Headmaster / Mistress	El / La director/a	dee-rek-tor/a
Interior decorator	El / La decorador/a	deh-koh-rah-dor/ah
Jeweller	El / La joyero/a	hoh-yeh-roh / rah
Journalist	El / La periodista	peh-ree-oh-dees-tah
Judge	El / la juez/a	hwehth/ah
Lawyer	El / La abogado/a	ah-boh-gah-doh / dah
Mechanic	El / La mecánico/a	meh-kah-nee-koh / kah
Musician	El / La músico/a	moo/-see-koh / kah
Nurse	El / La enfermero/a	en-fer-meh-roh / rah
Optician	El / la óptico/a	op-tee-koh / kah
Painter	El /La pintor/a	peen-tor/ah
Pharmacist	El / La farmacéutico/a	far-mah-theh-oo-tee-koh / kah
Photographer	El / La fotógrafo/a	foh-toh-grah-foh / fah
Physician	El / La médico/a	meh-dee-koh / kah
Pilot	El / La piloto	pee-loh-toh
Plasterer	El / La enlucidor/a	en-loo-thee-dor/ah

Learn Spanish In One Week

English	Spanish	Pronunciation
Plumber	El / La fontanero/a	fon-tah-neh-roh / rah
Policeman	El policía	poh-lee-thee-ah
President	El / La presidente/a	preh-see-den-teh / tah
Prime minister	El / La primer/a ministro/a	pree-mer/a-mee-nees-troh/trah
Producer	El / La productor/a	proh-dook-tor/ah
Psychologist	El / La psicólogo	see-koh-loh-goh / gah
Receptionist	El / La recepcionista	reh-thep-thee-oh-nees-tah
Salesman	El / La vendedor/a	ben-deh-dor/ah
Scientist	El / La cientifico/a	thee-en-tee-fee-koh / kah
Security guard	El / La guardia de seguridad	gwar-dee-ah-deh-seh-goo-ree-dad
Shop assistant	El / La vendedor/a	ben-deh-dor/ah
Soldier	El / La soldado/a	sol-dah-doh / dah
Solicitor	El / La abogado/a	ah-boh-gah-doh /dah
Sportsman / woman	El / la deportista	deh-por-tees-tah
Surgeon	El / La cirujano/a	thee-roo-hah-noh / nah
Teacher	El / La profesor/a	proh-feh-sor/ah
Train driver	El / La conductor/a del tren	kon-dook-tor/ah-del-tren
Waiter	El / La camarero/a	kah-mah-reh-roh / rah

Learn Spanish In One Week

GCSE Bonus Words / Useful Words

English	Spanish	Pronunciation
About	Aproximadamente	ah-prok-see-mah-dah-men-teh
Above	Encima de	en-thee-mah-deh
According to	Según	seh-goon
After	Después	des-pwehs
Again	Otra vez	oh-trah-beth
Against	Contra	kon-trah
Almost	Casi	kah-see
Already	Ya	yah
Also	También	tam-bee-en
Always	Siempre	see-em-preh
Among	Entre	en-treh
And	Y	ee
Are you free this weekend?	¿Estás libre este fin de semana?	es-tas-lee-breh-es-teh-feen-deh-seh-mah-nah
As well as	Además	ah-deh-mass
At	En	en
At the end of	Al final de	al-fee-nal-deh
Badly	Mal	mal
Because	Porque	por-keh
Because of	A causa de	ah-kow-sah-deh

Learn Spanish In One Week

English	Spanish	Pronunciation
Before	Antes	an-tehs
Behind	Detrás	deh-tras
Believe me	Créeme	kreh-eh-meh
Below / Down	Abajo	ah-bah-hoh
Best / Better	Mejor	meh-hor
Between	Entre	en-treh
Bitter	Amargo	ah-mar-goh
Bland	Soso	soh-soh
But	Pero	peh-roh
Come to my house	Ven a mi casa	ben-ah-mee-kah-sah
Disgusting	Asqueroso	ass-keh-roh-soh
Don't do it	No lo hagas	noh-loh-ah-gas
Don't do that	No hagas eso	noh-ah-gas-eh-soh
Don't even think about it	Ni se te ocurra	nee-seh-teh-oh-koo-rrah
Don't say that	No digas eso	noh-dee-gas-eh-soh
Don't worry about it	No pasa nada	noh-pah-sah-nah-dah
Don't you dare	Ni se te ocurra	nee-seh-teh-oh-koo-rrah
During	Durante	doo-ran-teh
Especially	Especialmente	es-peh-thee-al-men-teh

Learn Spanish In One Week

English	Spanish	Pronunciation
Everybody	Todo el mundo	toh-doh-el-moon-doh
Everyone	Todos	toh-dos
Everywhere	Por todas partes	por-toh-das-par-tehs
Except	Excepto	eks-thep-toh
Except	Salvo	sal-boh
Far (from)	Lejos	leh-hos
Few / Little / Not very	Poco	poh-koh
First of all	Lo primero	loh-pree-meh-roh
First time	Primera vez	pree-meh-rah-beth
For / In order to	Para	pah-rah
For a long time	Por mucho tiempo	por-moo-choh-tee-em-poh
For example	Por ejemplo	por-eh-hem-ploh
For how long	Para cuánto tiempo	pah-rah-kwan-toh-tee-em-poh
For how long	Por cuánto tiempo	por-kwan-toh-tee-em-poh
For what	Para qué	pah-rah-keh
Forget it	Olvídalo	ol-bee-dah-loh
Fortunately	Afortunadamente	ah-for-too-nah-dah-men-teh
Fortunately	Por suerte	por-swer-teh
From	De	deh
From	Desde	des-deh

Learn Spanish In One Week

English	Spanish	Pronunciation
Good morning / evening / night - (slang)	Buenas	bweh-nas
Good news	Buenas noticias	bweh-nas-noh-tee-thee-ass
He / She doesn't know	Él / Ella no sabe	el / eh-yah noh-sah-beh
Here	Aquí	ah-kee
Hot / Spicy	Picante	pee-kan-teh
However	Sin embargo	seen-em-bar-goh
How are you doing?	¿Cómo andamos?	koh-moh-an-dah-mos
How are you doing?	¿Cómo vas?	koh-moh-bas
How much does it cost?	¿Cuánto cuesta?	kwan-toh-kwes-tah
How much is it?	¿Cuánto es?	kwan-toh-es
How much is it worth?	¿Cuánto vale?	kwan-toh-bah-leh
How have you been?	¿Cómo has estado?	koh-moh-ass-es-tah-doh
How have you been?	¿Cómo te ha ido?	hoh-moh-teh-ah-ee-doh
How's it going?	¿Cómo vas?	koh-moh-bas
How old is he / she (are you)	¿Cuántos años tiene(s)?	kwan-tos-ah-nyohs-tee-eh-nehs
How would I know	Yo qué se	yoh-keh-seh
Hug me	Abrázame	ah-brah-thah-meh
Hug me	Abrazarme	ah-brah-thar-meh
I'm done	No puedo más	noh-pweh-doh-mas

Learn Spanish In One Week

English	Spanish	Pronunciation
I can relate	Comprendo perfectamente	kom-pren-doh-per-fek-tak-men-teh
I'm fed up	Estoy harto	es-toy-ar-toh
I'm going to work	Voy a trabajar	boy-ah-trah-bah-har
I'm on my way	Voy en camino	boy-en-kah-mee-noh
If	Si	see
In	En	en
In	Dentro de	den-troh-deh
In front of	Delante de	deh-lan-teh-deh
Inside	Dentro de	den-troh-deh
I'll be late sorry	Voy tarde lo siento	boy-tar-deh-loh-see-en-toh
I adore you	Te adoro	teh-ah-doh-roh
I don't get it	No lo pillo	noh-loh-pee-yoh
I don't have a clue	No tengo ni idea	noh-ten-goh-nee-ee-deh-ah
I don't have the slightest idea	No tengo la menor idea	noh-ten-goh-lah-meh-nor-ee-deh-ah
I don't have time for this	No tengo tiempo para esto	noh-ten-goh-tee-em-poh-pah-rah-es-toh
I don't understand you	No te entiendo	noh-teh-en-tee-en-doh
I get it	Entiendo	en-tee-en-doh
I love it	Me encanta	meh-en-kan-tah

Learn Spanish In One Week

English	Spanish	Pronunciation
I had a good time	La pasé bien	lah-pah-seh-bee-en
I had a good time	Me divertí	meh-dee-ber-tee
I had a good time	Pasé un buen rato	pah-seh-oon-bwen-rah-toh
I have no idea	No tengo ni idea	noh-ten-goh-nee-ee-deh-ah
I like you a lot	Me gustas mucho	meh-goos-tas-moo-choh
I need help	Necesito ayuda	neh-theh-see-toh-ah-yoo-dah
I need the bathroom	Necesito el baño	neh-theh-see-toh-el-bah-nyoh
I prefer	Prefiero	preh-fee-eh-roh
I really like you	Me encantas	meh-en-kan-tas
I really love you	Te quiero mucho	teh-kee-eh-roh-moo-choh
I swear	Juro	hoo-roh
I understand perfectly	Comprendo perfectamente	kon-pren-doh-per-fek-tah-men-teh
If	Si	see
I'm full	Estoy lleno/a	es-toy-yeh-noh / nah
I'm very full	Estoy llenísimo/a	es-toy-yeh-nee-see-moh / mah
Immediately	Inmediatamente	een-meh-dee-ah-tah-men-teh
In general	En general	en-heh-neh-ral
It escaped me	Se me fue	seh-meh-fweh
It's great	Está genial	es-tah-heh-nee-al
It's ok	No pasa nada	noh-pah-sah-nah-dah

Learn Spanish In One Week

English	Spanish	Pronunciation
It's on me	Yo invito	yoh-een-bee-toh
It's on the tip of my tongue	Lo tengo en la punta de la lengua	loh-ten-goh-en-lah-poon-tah-deh-lah-len-gwah
Kill the cockroach	Mata la cucaracha	mah-tah-lah-koo-kah-rah-chah
Kiss me	Bésame	beh-sah-meh
Less	Menos	meh-nos
Let me	Déjame	deh-hah-meh
Let me look	Déjame ver	deh-hah-meh-ber
Let me look for it	Déjame buscarlo	deh-hah-meh-boos-kar-loh
Like (similar) / As	Como	koh-moh
Long time	Mucho tiempo	moo-choh-tee-em-poh
Maximum	Máximo	mak-see-moh
Me neither	Yo tampoco	yoh-tam-poh-koh
Me too	Yo también	yoh-tam-bee-en
More	Más	mass
My mind's gone blank	Me he quedado en blanco	meh-eh-keh-dah-doh-en-blan-koh
Near / Near to	Cerca de	ther-kah-deh
Never mind	Olvídalo	ol-bee-dah-loh
Nevertheless	No obstante	noh-obs-tan-teh
Nevertheless	Sin embargo	seen-em-bar-goh

Learn Spanish In One Week

English	Spanish	Pronunciation
Next	Siguiente	see-gee-en-teh
Next to	Al lado de	al-lah-doh-deh
No good	No es bueno	noh-es-bweh-noh
No way	Para nada	pah-rah-nah-dah
No way	Qué va	keh-bah
Of course / It's clear	Está claro	es-tah-klah-roh
Of course	Por supuesto	por-soo-pwehs-toh
Of course / With out a doubt	Sin duda	seen-doo-dah
Often	A menudo	ah-meh-noo-doh
Older	Mayor	mah-yor
On	En	en
On	Sobre	soh-breh
On the corner of	En la esquina de	en-lah-es-kee-nah-deh
Once again	Otra vez	oh-trah-beth
Or	O	oh
Outside / Out of	Fuera de	dweh-rah-deh
Over there	Ahí	ah-ee
Perhaps	Quizás	kee-thas
Perhaps / Maybe	Tal vez	tal-beth

Learn Spanish In One Week

English	Spanish	Pronunciation
Quickly	Rápidamente	rrah-pee-dah-men-teh
Quickly / Fast	Rápido	rrah-pee-doh
Quite . Rather / Fairly	Bastante	bass-tan-teh
Really	Realmente	rreh-al-men-teh
Recently	Recientemente	rreh-thee-en-teh-men-teh
Right now	Ahora mismo	ah-oh-rah-mees-moh
Salty	Salado	sah-lah-doh
Same	Mismo	mees-moh
Same as / Equal to	igual a / igual de	ee-gwal-ah / ee-gwal-deh
Sickly	Empalagoso	em-pah-lah-goh-soh
Similar to	Parecido/a	pah-reh-thee-doh / dah
Since	Ya que	yah-keh
Since when	Desde cuándo	des-deh-kwan-doh
Sleep well	Que descanses	keh-des-kan-sehs
Someone	Alguien	al-gee-en
Something	Algo	al-goh
Sometimes	A veces	ah-beh-thehs
Sour	Agrio	ah-gree-oh
Still / Yet	Todavía	toh-dah-bee-ah

Learn Spanish In One Week

English	Spanish	Pronunciation
Straight away / immediately	En seguida	en-seh-gee-dah
Straight away / Right now	Ahora mismo	ah-oh-rah-mees-moh
Stop	Para	pah-rah
Stop / Halt	Alto	al-toh
Sure	Seguro	seh-goo-roh
Sure / yes	Claro	klah-roh
Sweet	Dulce	dool-theh
Take care	Cuídate	kwee-dah-teh
Tasteless	Insípido	een-see-pee-doh
The best	Lo mejor	loh-meh-hor
The majority	La mayoría	lah-mah-yoh-ree-ah
Then	Entonces	en-ton-thehs
Then / Next / Later	Luego	lweh-goh
They don't know	No saben	noh-sah-ben
Think	Cosa	koh-sah
Though / Even though	Aunque	ow-n-keh
Through	A través de	ah-trah-behs-deh
Through	Por	por
To	A	ah

Learn Spanish In One Week

English	Spanish	Pronunciation
Toward / Towards	Hacia	ah-thee-ah
Too	Demasiado	deh-mah-see-ah-doh
Under	Bajo	bah-hoh
Under	Debajo de	deh-bah-hoh-deh
Unfortunately	Desafortunadamente	des-ah-for-too-nah-dah-men-teh
Until	Hasta	ass-tah
Up there	Arriba	ah-rree-bah
Very	Muy	mwee
We don't know	No sabemos	noh-sah-beh-moss
Well	Bien	bee-en
Well worth seeing	Vale la pena ver	bah-leh-lah-peh-nah-ber
What are you doing tonight?	¿Qué haces esta noche?	keh-ah-thehs-es-tah-noh-cheh
What are you saying?	¿Qué dices?	keh-dee-thehs
What colour?	¿De qué color?	deh-keh-koh-lor
What date?	¿Qué fecha?	keh-feh-chah
What day?	¿Qué día?	keh-dee-ah
What did you say?	¿Qué has dicho?	keh-ass-dee-choh
What happened?	¿Qué pasó?	keh-pah-soh

Learn Spanish In One Week

English	Spanish	Pronunciation
What have you done? / made?	¿Qué has hecho?	keh-ass-eh-choh
What's new?	¿Qué hay de nuevo?	keh-eye-deh-nweh-boh
What's up?	¿Qué hay?	keh-eye
What's new? / What's up?	¿Qué hay de nuevo?	keh-eye-deh-nweh-boh
What's up? / What's new?	¿Qué me cuentas?	keh-meh-kwen-tas
What's wrong?	¿Qué pasa?	keh-pah-sah
Where is it?	¿Dónde está?	don-deh-es-tah
Which day?	¿Qué día?	keh-dee-ah
With	Con	kon
With love	Con amor	kon-ah-mor
With pleasure	Con mucho gusto	kon-moo-choh-goos-toh
Without	Sin	seen
Why not?	¿Por qué no?	por-keh-noh
Worse	Peor	peh-or
Wrong number	El número equivocado	el-noo-meh-roh-eh-kee-boh-kah-doh
Yeah I'm almost there	Si ya estoy llegando	see-yah-es-toy-yeh-gan-doh
Yeah right	Sí claro	see-klah-roh
You're such a pain	Eres un pesado	eh-rehs-oon-peh-sah-doh

Summary

I hope you enjoy this book and refer to it time and time again to improve your Spanish language skills. Spanish is the second most spoken language in the world and learning Spanish can create many opportunities, help with your career, enhance your travel experiences, boost your employment prospects and increase your confidence.

You must practise daily and say the words and phrases out loud. Don't be shy and talk to everyone in Spanish. You'll be surprised how quickly you advance and how good you become and sound.

Best wishes!

Geoff Jackson

March 2023

Printed in Dunstable, United Kingdom